Easy Songs *for* Smooth TRANSITIONS
in the Classroom

NINA ARAÚJO
CAROL AGHAYAN

Redleaf Press®
www.redleafpress.org
800-423-8309

Published by Redleaf Press
10 Yorkton Court
St. Paul, MN 55117
www.redleafpress.org

Lyrics to "Good Morning, How Are You?" "Everybody Shake a Hand," "Only One Can Talk at a Time," "Tidy Up," and "Get On Board, Little Children" by Jean Feldman. Reprinted with permission.

Lyrics to "Sit on Your Bottom" by Margaret Sansovich. Reprinted with permission.

Every effort has been made to locate, contact, and acknowledge copyright owners. If we have inadvertently omitted acknowledgment of copyright ownership, we ask that you please contact us at the above address.

First edition 2006
Cover design by Jim Handrigan
Cover image © Fancy Collection/Veer
Interior typeset in ITC Legacy Sans Book
Interior illustrations by Becky Radtke
Printed in the United States of America
21 20 19 18 17 16 15 14   6 7 8 9 10 11 12 13

Library of Congress Cataloging-in-Publication Data

Araújo, Nina.
    Easy songs for smooth transitions in the classroom / Nina Araújo and Carol Aghayan.— 1st ed.
        p. cm.
    Includes index.
    ISBN 978-1-929610-83-9
    1. School music—Instruction and study. 2. Music—Handbooks, manuals, etc.   I. Aghayan,
    Carol. II. Title.
    MT10.A86 2006
    372.87'3—dc22

                                                      2005028685

Printed on acid-free paper

To Susannah Stone Eldridge, with love and admiration for so many young lives that were forever touched by a phenomenal educator.

—Nina

This book is dedicated to the Early Childhood Education students at the Louisiana Technical College and Louisiana State University who have inspired me for over twenty years.

—Carol

Contents

Acknowledgments

Every book is a celebration of the work of many people who make such projects possible. I would like to thank Susannah Eldridge, an extraordinary woman who inspired me greatly in the early years in my career. With much patience and wisdom, she guided my steps and touched my life forever.

This book echoes the stories of all the children and their families who helped me understand what every child needed to have a positive experience in my care. I thank them for teaching me about the world of early childhood.

I could not have worked with children for so many years without the contributions of volunteers, undergraduate students, and graduate students who taught me about daily rediscovering early childhood with the challenge of so many unanswered questions.

Loving family, friends, and colleagues read the early version of this manuscript and were very gracious with their recommendations. I want to especially thank my sister, Rita Araújo, for reading the manuscript in English and giving me advice in Portuguese.

I want to thank Debbie LeeKeenan from Eliot-Pearson Children's School, the preschool laboratory school at Tufts University, for helping me grow in my role as a teacher with her admirable and dedicated mentoring.

Our editor, Beth Wallace, with inspiring patience and sound advice, offered intelligent and creative ideas while helping us reflect on the mission of this book. To her, thanks for such encouragement and spark!

A very dedicated educator inspired me with such a humble approach to valuing contributions from young and seasoned professionals in the field of early childhood education. David Dickinson taught me about believing in people's potential to grow.

Three very dedicated women supported me while I worked on this book by helping me transition one of my sons into life in preschool while spending a summer in Middlebury, Vermont. Dhyanna Darden, Lori Nicklaw, and Stacy Stevens were exceptional with Luc and his first experience in group care at age four.

Many people helped me with words of encouragement that made a difference in how I immersed myself in this honorable task: Janie Starks from Partnerships in Child Care/Volunteers of America, for welcoming me into that family of committed educators in Baton Rouge, Louisiana; Jane Cassidy, who offered access to her personal collection of books and research journals in the field of early childhood research and music and trusted us with materials that were invaluable to this project; Bill Kelley, who donated his time and equipment to record the first demo companion audio recording for this project; Zirque Bonner, for his guidance, patience, creative talent, and advice during the recording sessions for the final CD; Paul Stein, an accomplished author and educator for his dear encouragement especially during the last portion of this project; Tom Hunter, who shared hopeful messages to keep going and sharing songs with others in our field.

Thanks to my young sons, Luc and André, for their creative adaptation of all the songs in this book, and their supportive hugs, kisses, and love notes at the end of the day! A good portion of this book was written after hours, with the exceptional and nurturing support of my husband, Michael Kerry. He has patiently read many versions of this book and contributed sound advice and patient editing; without his continued encouragement and honest critiques over the last five years, this book would not exist!

Finally, my most special thank you goes to my father, Geraldo Araújo, for supporting my calling to keep teaching young children and training young teachers, and for welcoming early mornings with "O Sol No Céu Brilhou."

—Nina Araújo

Thanks and gratitude to Diane Burts for sharing her songs, her expertise, and her heart with me and hundreds of ECE (Early Childhood Education) students over the last thirty years. Warmest thanks go to my dear friends and colleagues Gwen Marks, Janie Starks, Betty Blaize, Joan Benedict, Terry Buchannan, and Sarah Pierce for supporting and encouraging me. Thanks to Jane Cassidy for her guidance and encouragement as we began this process. I am so grateful to Dr. Jean Feldman, for sharing her songs and inspiration, and to Bev Bos, for affecting my teaching and music at so many levels.

My unending appreciation goes to all the teachers and young children who tried out our songs in their classrooms so we could share our love of music with them.

On a more personal level, thanks to my dear husband Mike for managing to love, support, and encourage me throughout this three-year-long endeavor. For my children, Ashley and Christopher, thank you for enduring hundreds of hours of children's music without complaint. And for Maw Maw Bev, thank you for filling our lives with music and happy thoughts.

—Carol Aghayan

Introduction

If you can walk you can dance;
If you can talk, you can sing

—Zimbabwean Proverb

Singing has become a very risky activity these days. In our culture, where the pressure to perform reaches all the way down to preschool, most of us choose to push a button on a CD player and let the professionals make the music that we hear. Videos and DVDs have replaced the homespun music traditions once integral to family life. Our peers often judge us very harshly and express their opinions ungraciously. Childhood music—created by parents and children, for children—has been replaced by TV show jingles. Sadly, even children have come to think that music is best left to professionals. They need adults who are unafraid to sing for them and with them.

Singing is in fact one of the best things that we can do with children. From birth, babies are biologically primed to respond with pleasure to human voice (Honig 1995). Notice the singsong way in which caregivers speak to their infants and how the infants respond to it. Music reduces stress by allowing us to relax and be silly, while requiring us to be open to improvisation and encouraging physical and emotional closeness. Music encourages us to use our whole bodies while also stimulating our minds and satisfying our emotions. When we make singing a habit, the numerous repetitions of our favorite songs engrave them permanently in our memories and carry along the associated positive memories of the people in our lives who sang with us. Singing builds relationships; when we sing together, we feel that we belong with each other.

Children are the best possible audience for shy singers because they care less about the "beauty" of our voices or if we sing perfectly in key than about when (often!) and especially what (songs that they can understand and relate to) we choose to sing with them. Appropriately chosen songs make children feel how extraordinary each of them is in our eyes; music involves them in a way that often nothing else does. Singing together is a reliable recipe for spending quality time with our children and developing secure, trusting relationships within the group: one of the best gifts a teacher can give a child.

Since we are aware of the great benefits of singing, it is worth remembering that children, bombarded by media messages that say singing is best left to the professionals, can only learn about using music in everyday life if we make music with them often. Transitions, a much-neglected aspect of daily school life, are a great time to incorporate singing. Often our hands are busy, and during those few seconds or few minutes of downtime as we shift focus, we lose momentum, allowing behavior issues to develop. Singing focuses both the singers and the listeners, particularly when the song grabs the children's attention by using their names or referring to common experiences and favorite objects. Many times we can even use songs that relate to the upcoming activity, helping the children anticipate it. While no substitute for careful planning and consideration of the needs and temperaments of children, singing is a great "glue" that helps to hold things together during the day.

The songs in this book offer an alternative-musical-approach for transitions in the classroom. We have included music that helps children regroup, shift focus, and move forward while maintaining their connection to each other, their teachers, and the day's events. We suggest using music that is about participation and not performance. We discourage the use of recorded music for transitions, because recorded music can't incorporate the names of all our children, is unchanging and thus inflexible, is often inconvenient and distracting, and frequently discourages participation. The songs in this publication, carefully selected and field-tested, elicit joyful participation from children and have been used with success in many settings. We are indebted to many very small people for sharing their strong opinions about our choice of songs!

As you read this book, look for opportunities to adapt the ideas and material to your particular experience and setting. Every child and schedule will be different every year, as students and colleagues come and go. You alone know what to do to make each song sound as if it belongs to your group or to a specific child in your classroom.

Although we advocate taking the time to sit down and carefully consider your day and plan for transitions, we realize that many teachers will not have the time or desire to do so. In this case, we would like to suggest that you start slowly—adding a song or chant here or there during the day, particularly songs useful for waiting periods—and then evaluating what worked before investing more time and effort. We're confident that you'll find that your efforts are rewarded many times over, with happier, calmer transitions.

Lastly and most importantly, don't be shy; just sing! The more you sing, the more you will like it, and the more your children will like it. As Ruth Crawford Seeger used to say, "Carry the song around with you, as children do" (Seeger 2002).

What Do We Mean by "Transition"?

When we talk about transitions, we usually think about two types of transitions: life transitions, such as getting married, having a child, moving, starting a new job; and transitions that we experience daily, such as waking up, going to work, going to school, getting ready to sleep. *Easy Songs for Smooth Transitions in the Classroom* addresses the latter type. More specifically, we use transition to refer to the time between two activities, routines, or places during the day (for example, from home to school, between free choice and circle time, or between snack and outdoor playtime).

During a typical group care day we experience on average nine daily transitions for a half-day program and from sixteen to twenty in a full-day program. At five to ten minutes per transition, this translates to one and a half to three hours per day! We carefully plan the rest of the school day; why should transitions be any different? When we teach teachers to use music for transitions, we often hear comments such as, "'It's so simple, why didn't I think of doing this before?" or "It's so easy and it makes all the difference in the world when I plan for it! There are so many of them, I cannot believe that I never paid attention to them."

Transitions represent change—change of activity, energy level, space, or focus. Change can be difficult for all of us, but especially for young children. Teachers and children alike need to prepare for upcoming changes. Without preparation, the seemingly small times "in-between" can be chaotic and stressful. Planning for those moments can minimize or eliminate problems; when everyone knows what is happening, how and when, and what their roles are, we can avoid unnecessary stress. Children feel in control and empowered to participate when they know what is happening next; they need to be reminded of this in a familiar, comfortable, and playful way. In this way we can transform transitions into a safety net, so that they become the glue that holds the day together.

We've identified seven different types of transitions:

- Greetings and good-byes
- Gatherings and dismissals
- Calling attention
- Cleaning up
- Moving
- Waiting
- Slowing down

Each transition requires a different kind of mood and song. However, many songs are flexible enough to be used for several different transitions. It's up to you to get to know your children and use the songs that best fit each child and your group as a whole.

What Makes Transitions Smooth?

Music during transitions is not a magic wand. Although music can soften the edges, it is no substitute for thoughtful attention to planning in our programs. Creating smooth transitions requires a multifaceted approach: strong teacher-child relationships, an orderly environment, and a well-balanced and predictable schedule are all important contributors to smooth transitions. In addition, before we can use music effectively, we need to "get in tune" with each child. Only then can we find a song that will keep all the children interested and engaged, helping them succeed in their efforts to transition from one part of the day to another.

The Caregiver's Voice

Our relationships with children are the most important factor in smooth transitions. And strong relationships are built on what is familiar, predictable, and safe. Regardless of what your voice sounds like, it is the connection through music you make with each child in your group that is important and encourages rich, healthy development. For this reason, the tracks on the CD that comes with this book are very short. The CD is not included for use in the classroom. It is meant as an aid to help you, the caregiver, learn the songs and chants.

We are aware that for some of you using your own voice instead of a CD will be challenging. However, you can carry your voice with you wherever you go, and it is infinitely more flexible. For the children, your voice is the most familiar sound in the classroom. It has a stronger influence on them than any recorded music. Here are other reasons why we don't advise you to play the CD that comes with this book in your classroom:

- When you use your voice, you can adapt and stretch the songs to fit your context.
- You can stop and start easily.
- Only you know the children's names and can incorporate them into the songs.
- You can adjust the tempo (speed) of each song to any situation, in order to encourage your children to participate. Mostly this means slow down! A tempo appropriate for toddlers is generally slower than one for preschoolers.
- The songs on the CD are much shorter than you would want to use in the classroom—they are merely samples to help you learn the songs more easily.
- You are the only one who can emphasize a certain word that has a special meaning.
- You can adapt songs to fit your children's family contexts and incorporate a local twist to them such as, "Cleaning up is wicked fun!" (Boston

area); "Tchau, Tchau" (André's family from Brazil); "Are y'all ready?" (Ashley's family from Louisiana); "¡Hasta la vista!" (Ana's family from Guatemala); etc.

To get started, you can always chant a song and gradually add clapping and the melody. Practice, practice, practice, and make it yours. Use the same song for a while for transitions like cleaning up, greeting, and saying good-bye. This book offers several songs for each transition so that you can choose what works best for you and the children (don't worry, they will give you immediate feedback on the songs they like!).

Schedules for Young Children

Understanding transitions can be challenging without knowing how a schedule works. Much like the art of weaving a basket, all activities and routines need to follow an order and keep children feeling that they are an important part of the group. Your schedule for the day needs to be developmentally appropriate, to have a balanced combination of active and quiet play, and to flow throughout the day with carefully planned transitions. Quite the task for novice and seasoned teachers alike!

Some schedules are dictated by the administration of the program; some of them are determined by teachers in the classroom. There are schedules for half- and full-day attendance and for various ages from infancy to grade school. Schedules for infants and toddlers usually revolve around the children's needs and are very flexible. As children get older, we encourage them to adapt to more regular and communal routines. Schedules determine how many transitions we will end up with at the end of the day. They need to be flexible yet predictable, and for that reason, transition songs should be the same.

We define daily activities as the parts of the schedule that can and do change as the year progresses (for example, reading stories, free-play time, a visit to a local art studio for pottery activities). We refer to daily routines as the parts of the day that don't change, such as breakfast, snack, and lunch times, toileting, brushing teeth, taking a nap. These need to be realistic, familiar, and predictable. Planning daily schedules requires differentiating daily activities and daily routines. It is a balancing act to make sure that neither one is programmed to happen at inconvenient times, too often, or infrequently.

Here are some suggestions for creating a balanced schedule:

- Use a variety of experiences and activity levels to accommodate children's special needs, temperaments, and developmental stages.
- Plan for a healthy balance between teacher-directed and child-initiated activities.
- Include a variety of activity levels that alternate and follow one another. Outside activities should precede a quiet indoor activity like shared reading.
- Adapt your schedule to grow and change as children get older.

- Be realistic. For example, rarely do we clean up the whole room in ten minutes.
- Minimize your transition times as the seasons change. For example, in the winter, greet the children outside, and allow them to play in the snow first, if changing in and out of snow gear adds stress or if it shortens inside playtime.
- Use your Transition Planning Guide to plan transitions (see Appendix C).

Getting Started

Although in an ideal world all teachers would have adequate time to plan for transitions, most teachers have little or no planning time. Our goal is to make your day run more smoothly, but we cannot offer a magic bullet. We suggest that you start gradually, targeting the most challenging transition you have in your day. As teachers ourselves, we find that the most challenging transitions are greeting (as we manage children's anxieties about leaving their caregivers at the beginning of the day), cleaning up (as we ask them to interrupt the flow of their play and switch focus in a short amount of time), and waiting times (when they become restless and confused about the flow of the day). It may make sense to begin with a song or two that will help with your most challenging transition. Alternately, you might find a song that you like or that sticks in your head. Learn it well, and then use it during a transition for which it is suited.

You'll find a set of song cards for all the songs at the end of the book. You can photocopy these onto labels and stick them on file cards. Punch a hole in the corner and put your favorite songs on a key ring. Then when you notice that a transition is becoming stressful, you can draw on a favorite song to ease the way.

In the song lyrics, words that are surrounded by square brackets [like this] can be replaced to adapt the lyrics to your own needs, your classroom routines, and your children. The words in the brackets are just examples; change them to make the songs work for you!

When you do use a song, note your children's reactions. Jot down a few notes on your song card to help you improve the experience next time. Be open to the benefits of using music especially during difficult transitions. We're confident that you will be happily surprised!

References and Resources

Baker, Amy C., and Lynn A. Manfredi/Petitt. 2004. *Relationships, the heart of quality care: Creating community among adults in early care settings.* Washington, D.C.: National Association for the Education of Young Children.

Bredekamp, Sue, and Carol Copple, eds. 1997. *Developmentally appropriate practice in early childhood programs.* Revised Edition. Washington, D.C.: National Association for the Education of Young Children.

Buckoff, Rita. 1994. Joyful noises: Facilitating language growth through the rhythmic response to chants. *Young Children* (May 1994): 26–30.

Feierabend, John. 1986. *Music for very little people: 50 playful activities for infants and toddlers.* Farmingdale, N.Y.: Boosey & Hawkes.

Gagne, Denise. 1997. *Singing games children love.* Vol. 2. Red Deer, Alberta, Canada: Themes & Variations.

Hayes, Kathleen, and Renée Creange. 2001. *Classroom routines that really work for pre-k and kindergarten.* New York, N.Y.: Scholastic Professional Books.

Honig, Alice Sterling. 1995. Singing with infants and toddlers. *Young Children* (July 1995): 72–78.

Larson, Nola, Mary Henthorne, and Barbara Plum. 1994. *Transition magician: Strategies for guiding young children in early childhood programs.* St. Paul, Minn.: Redleaf.

Lerner, Claire, and Lynette Ciervo. 2002. Getting in tune: The powerful influence of music on young children's development. www.zerotothree.org.

Moore, Thomas. 2002. If you teach children, you can sing. *Young Children* (July 2002): 84–85.

Seeger, Ruth Crawford. 2002. *American folksongs for children.* New York: Oak Publications.

———. 1950. *Animal folksongs for children.* Garden City, N.Y.: Doubleday.

Wirth, Marian, Verna Stassevitch, Rita Shotwell, and Patricia Stemmler. 1983. *Musical games, fingerplays, and rhythmic activities for early childhood.* West Nyack, N.Y.: Parker.

YMCA of the USA, Dartmouth Medical School, and Institute for American Values. 2003. Hardwired to connect: The new scientific case for authoritative communities. A report to the nation from the Commission on Children at Risk.

Greetings and Good-byes

The children arrive in Ms. Breaux's classroom at different times in the morning. When Ashley comes in with her mother, Ms. Breaux makes eye contact with her at the door, then kneels down and greets Ashley by singing a verse from a familiar song—"Hello, Ashley, yes, indeed" (CD track 3). Still looking at Ashley, Ms. Breaux adds, "I'm so glad you came to school today, Ashley! We've been waiting for you!" She then proceeds to greet Ashley's mom.

Ms. Breaux plans for greeting children individually each morning because she knows that the first few moments at school set the tone for the rest of the day and are critical to providing continuity in children's lives. Ms. Breaux always uses known songs, chants, or a rhyme that includes every child's name, because she knows from experience that these predictable and familiar rituals make each child feel special and included. All the children hear, "Hello! We know you, and we like you. You are welcome here."

At the other end of a long day, Ashley and Ms. Breaux are both tired. Ms. Breaux is sitting on the floor with Ashley and a few other children. Ms. Breaux sees Ashley's mother coming through the door and starts singing, "Good-bye, Ashley, hey, hey" (CD track 9) as Ashley reunites with her mom at the end of the day. The song signals whose parent is at the door and provides reassurance that Ms. Breaux will be waiting for them at school the next day.

Leo is sitting on the rug with Ms. Breaux and Ashley, but his day is not over yet: he goes to an after-school program at a neighbor's house. Ms. Breaux plans her good-byes to Leo differently. She lets him know about what the classroom curriculum looks like the next day. She often asks him to help set up one of the activities for the next morning, thereby reassuring him that his routine at school is safe and predictable while also giving him something to look forward to. When Leo's father comes through the door, Ms. Breaux sings "Hasta la vista, Leo, hey, hey," using words from the language his family speaks at home (Spanish).

Good Morning to You

Unknown Source | CD Track 1 | Song Card Page 98

       G   C   G

[Good morning, good morning], [good morning] to you,

               G7   D7   G

[Good morning] to [someone] who's [wearing the color blue].

       G   C   G

[Good morning, good morning], [good morning] to you,

               G7   D7   G

[Good morning] to [Ashley], who's wearing the color [yellow].

Using the Song

Greeting children as they arrive with this song is a great way to set the tone for the rest of the day. Likewise, if you want to use this song at the end of the day, use it to reassure children and their families that their teachers and friends will be happy to see them again soon. These very important times contribute to strengthening relationships with the children and their families.

Use this time to connect with individual children by singing a verse to each child as they put away their belongings. Some children might need more than a verse to feel comfortable and transition into the day while they separate from their caregiver. Sing the song to the caregiver as well, if you feel that some children may benefit from it.

Variations

- Use the last line of the song to highlight concepts that are meaningful to them (for example, "Good morning to someone whose name begins with A"—in this case, to a child named Ashley).
- Invite children to take turns leading the song.
- This song can be used at gathering times, as you give children time to finish individual projects before they are ready to fully transition into the next activity (for example, cleaning up, gluing the last piece of wood in a collage project, washing hands, etc.).
- During morning gathering, add information to the words that describe specific children and invite them to guess who you are singing about (for example, "Good morning to someone who likes to play with worms").

Good Morning, How Are You?

CD Track 2 | Song Card Page 98

(Tune: "If You're Happy and You Know It")

      D   A7   D

[Good morning], [Emillie]. How are you? [Good morning], [Emillie]. How are you?

   G   D   Bm   G   A7   D

It will be a [special] day, I'm so glad you came to play. [Good morning], [Emillie]. How are you?

   D   A7   D

[Bonjour], [Simone]. How are you? [Bonjour], [Simone]. How are you?

   G   D   Bm G A7   D

It will be a [happy] day, I'm so glad you came to play. [Bonjour], [Simone]. How are you?

   D   A7   D   A7

[Salaam], [Omeed]. How are you? [Salaam], [Omeed]. How are you?

   G   D   Bm G A7   D

It will be a [rainy] day, I'm so glad you came to play. [Salaam], [Omeed]. How are you?

Using the Song

When you sing this song, invite the children to help you make every day special. It is particularly valuable to call their attention with welcoming words, such as, "I'm so glad you came to play." At times, you will find that you need to add a short pause after you sing this line to give certain children extra time to let the message settle. Regardless of how challenging the previous day was, this song can help them start a new day, with new goals and fresh emotions. Children who are having a hard time separating and adapting to group care routines may also benefit from this song to emphasize "new beginnings."

Learn how to greet children in their home language, or make up your very own way to greet each child at the beginning of each day (some teachers have nicknames for each child). Make sure you ask their families for the accurate words (for example, "Bom dia" means "good morning" in Portuguese, but four-year-old André greets people at home by saying "Tudo bem?" instead).

Variations

- In line 3 use different ways of inviting children to make each day special. After a while, pause at that point and let them fill in the blanks and tell you what kind of day it will be ("It will be an exciting day"; "It will be a brand new day").
- Use two names at once, if drop-off times tend to be busy, so you can acknowledge every child individually (for example, "Good morning, Emily and Catara. How are you?").
- Use humor to elicit a response from children ("I'm so glad you came to feed the worms"; "I'm so glad you came to splash in puddles.").
- Use this song at the beginning of large group time and invite children to shake hands, wave hello, and use various forms of greetings to say "hi" to one another.

Lyrics by Jean Feldman. Reprinted with permission.

Hello, Everybody, Yes, Indeed

Traditional Folk Song | CD Track 3 | Song Card Page 98

G   D7   G
Oh [hello], [everybody], yes, indeed. Yes, indeed. Yes, indeed.

G   C   D7   G
Oh [hello], [everybody], yes, indeed. Yes, indeed, [my darling]!

G   D7   G
Oh [hello], [Hesakai], yes, indeed. Yes, indeed. Yes, indeed.

G   C   D7   G
Oh [hello], [Shante], yes, indeed. Yes, indeed, [my darling]!

G   D7   G
[Buenos Dias], [Manuel], yes, indeed. Yes, indeed. Yes, indeed.

G   C   D7   G
[Buenos Dias], [Manuel], yes, indeed. Yes, indeed, [my darling]!

Using the Song

This song's repetitive verses help the children transition into their morning routine. They can quickly predict what subsequent verses will sound like without having to process too much new information as they separate from their caregivers and start a new day. Use a culturally acceptable form of welcoming each child to help him or her feel at ease in your classroom (wave hello, rub backs, give high fives, hug, etc.). Sing to family members, too, as they also need a special greeting in the morning. Ask individual children how they would like to be greeted and incorporate this information into the song.

Variations

- Use this song for the beginning of a circle time.
- Ask the children to add something ("Who else can we say hello to?"; "How can we say hello to you, Abdul?"; "How do you say 'hello' or 'good morning' at your house, Yeh-Eun?").
- Use this song to invite children to join you and their peers as you transition from free play to whole group meetings.
- Ask children for various types of body movements to add to this song (for example, hand clapping, head bobbing, chest slapping). For older children, add on additional movements to the ones they are currently doing. With younger children, do one motion at a time.

Sally, Go 'Round the Sun

Traditional | Adapted by Nina Araújo | CD Track 4 | Song Card Page 98

[Celia] go 'round the [sun],

[Celia] go 'round the moon,

[Celia], [good morning] to you, [my friend],

We'll play together soon!

[Anna] go 'round the sun,

[Anna] go 'round the moon,

[Anna], [good morning] to you, [my friend],

We'll play [with puzzles] soon!

Using the Song

This short chant is a great way to slowly greet children early in the morning. Use some silly words in place of sun to quickly connect with children ("Celia go 'round the ceiling, Celia go 'round the rooftop," etc.). Use this song as an opportunity to ease each child through the transition into the day. Name one activity that you know will entice him or her to engage with the classroom environment and will bring familiar memories from the day before or from a comfortable experience from any given day for continuity.

Variations

- You can chant with the same line, if this makes more sense to start with:
  "[Celia], good morning to you, [Celia], good morning to you,
  [Celia], good morning to you, [my friend], we'll play together soon!"
- You can easily adapt this chant to be used at the end of the day as well:
  [Celia] go 'round the sun, [Celia] go 'round the moon,
  [Celia], [good-bye] to you, [my friend], we'll see each other soon!

I'm Glad You Came Out Today

Traditional | Adapted by Carol Aghayan | CD Track 5 | Song Card Page 98
(Tune: "Buffalo Gals")

   A   E7   A
[Marwan O'Kiell] I'm glad you came out today, came out today, came out today.

                                E7   A
[Marwan O'Kiell] I'm glad you came out today, 'cause we're gonna [have some fun].

 A   E7   A
[Bella Rose] I'm glad you came out today, came out today, came out today.

                            E7   A
[Bella Rose] I'm glad you came out today, 'cause we're gonna [play with blocks].

 A   E7   A
[Lakeitha Brown] I'm glad you came out today, came out today, came out today.

                            E7   A
[Lakeitha Brown] I'm glad you came out today, 'cause we're gonna [take a walk].

Using the Song

When children hear a teacher sing "I'm glad you came out today," they learn about how caring adults other than their parents relate to them in the world outside their homes.

You have a great opportunity to personalize this song with information for each child. Spend time observing children during the day to learn what each child likes to do in the classroom and incorporate that information into the song (for example, "'cause we're gonna play with blocks"). Knowing what helps them connect with you might help children who are adapting to new teachers, environments, and other children in the classroom.

Sometimes using each child's first and last name can be a mouthful. Instead, you can simply sing, "My dear Hamish, I'm glad you came out today."

Variations

- When two children, or more, arrive at the same time, use as many names as you can fit in each verse:

  "Stacy and Hamdi, I'm glad you came out today."

  "Stacy, Hamdi, and Ivan, I'm glad you came out today."

Hickory Dickory Dock

Traditional | Adapted by Nina Araújo | CD Track 6 | Song Card Page 98

      F
[Hickory Dickory Dock], [Annieck] ran up the clock.

                    Bb
The clock struck [one], [Annieck] went home,

   C7   F
[Hickory Dickory Dock].

Using the Song

Many older preschoolers are developing an interest in time and the order of events in one day. This song is good for indicating the time to go home (when the clock strikes). Use it to say good-bye to individual children before they go home. You can also ask them for "good-bye clock sounds" to personalize this song beyond using their names.

Variations

- To add humor and to play with initial sounds, change the first letters in the phrase "Hickory Dickory Dock" (for example, "Pickory Pickory Pock").
- Use this song to dismiss and transition children into other activities, such as going outside or eating snacks ("The clock struck ten, Wesley went out"; "The clock struck 9:30, Sophie ate her snack").

Good-bye; Don't Cry

Traditional | CD Track 7 | Song Card Page 98

     D   G   A7   D
Good-bye. [Don't cry.] [Wipe a tear from your eye.]

     G   D   A7   D
Cheery up [ching ching]. Good-bye, old thing. Boom diddy ah good-bye.

     D   G   A7   D
Before you go, I want you to know

     G   D   A7   D
It's been such fun, [The things we've done], boom diddy ah good-bye.

Using the Song

This song helps provide closure at the end of the day and sets the stage for children to remember some of the fun things they did at school so they can share their experiences with parents and caregivers upon departure. It is always a good idea to include children's names at the beginning of the song (for example, "Good-bye, dear Kira, it's time to say good-bye").

This song also helps children remember what they did during the day ("It's been such fun, we played with worms"; "It's been such fun, we went to King's Garden"). Use this song as an opportunity to highlight positive experiences and help children with beginning-of-the-year transitions.

Variations

- Help children anticipate the next day by asking them "what fun things" they will do. Include it in your planning for the next day to help with drop-off transitions.
- Use the first letter in each child's name to sing the "ching, ching" part (for example, "Good-bye, dear Pedro, wipe a tear from your eye, cheery up ping, ping.").
- Modify the second line to offer reassurance and a sense of routine ("Good-bye, dear Olga, we'll see you again tomorrow"; "Good-bye, dear Rati, we'll be waiting for you tomorrow.").
- If you choose to sing the song without adaptations, encourage children to say good-bye to one another as they sing this song.

Greetings and Good-byes

What Shall We Do When We Go Home?

Traditional | Adapted by Nina Araújo | CD Track 8 | Song Card Page 98

E   A   B7   E
What shall [Don] do when [he] [goes home]? What shall [Don] do when [he] [goes home]?

E7   A   B7   E
What shall [Don] do when [he] [goes home]? When [he] goes [home today]?

E   A   E   A
[He'll have a snack] when [he] goes home. [He'll have a snack] when [he] goes home.

E   A   B7   E
[He'll have a snack] when [he] goes home. When [he] goes [home today].

Using the Song

Use this song to help children find something to look forward to doing after they leave school. Be sensitive to the fact that not all children will necessarily go straight home after being in child care for a portion of the day; some children may go to after-school care, their grandparents' house, or another child care center. Ask individual children what they do when they leave school, and incorporate this information into the song. The words also teach young children about home rituals and traditions. Leave enough time to listen to your children's answers. When you first use this song, it might take a while for children to sing with you. It is often difficult for young children to sequence daily events and anticipate what they'll do when they go home. In those cases, try to find out about their favorite dinner foods or popular home activities to help them in their transitions back to home routines. Leave enough time for listening to children's answers.

Variations

- Encourage children to look forward to returning to school by singing, "What shall we do when we come back? When we come back tomorrow?"; or "When we come back to Otter Creek Child Center?"
- You can adapt this song to fit many transitions:
  - **Moving:** "What shall Nadine do when she's outside?"
  - **Dismissal:** "What shall Mara do at free choice time?"
  - **Clean up:** "What shall Van do at clean-up time?"; "She'll wash off the table at clean-up time."
- Try using something absurd or out of the ordinary to encourage children to participate (for example, "She'll wash a car when she goes home"; "He'll feed his elephant when he goes home").

Good-bye, Hey, Hey

Traditional | Adapted by Nina Araújo | CD Track 9 | Song Card Page 98
(Tune: "Little Lap-Dog Lullaby")

    F   Bb   F   Bb
[Good-bye], Katherine, [hey, hey]. [Tchau, tchau], Mônica, [hey, hey].

    F   Bb   F   Bb
[Good-bye], Ella, [hey, hey]. [Á bientôt], Juliette, [hey, hey].

      F   Bb   F
We're gonna be right here when you come back,

      F   Bb   F
We're gonna be right here when you come back,

      F   Bb   F
We're gonna be right here when you come back,

               Bb   F
Go'n' to be so happy here to see you back again.

Using the Song

This very simple song is a good way to acknowledge each child individually while reassuring him or her that though the day has ended, a new one is coming soon. Ask children how they would like to be wished good-bye and incorporate this into the song. The second part of this song sends a consistent and repetitive message to children: we will always be here when you come back to school. Many children have unpredictable schedules after they leave their school environment, and it is important to provide a safety net to them: "No matter what changes in your house tonight, your teachers will be here at the same place and with the same smile to greet you in the morning."

Variations

- Make up different sounds to substitute for "hey, hey."
- Use a variety of words for "hey, hey" (for example, "Good-bye, Ella, hugs, hugs").
- Hum the "hey, hey" parts instead (for example, "Hello, Ella, hmm, hmm").
- Try using this song for greeting and change the words to fit that transition:

  Hello, Ella, hey, hey. (4X)

  It's so good to see you here today. (4X)
- If you use this song for greeting your children, you can also make up a line that talks about what they are wearing that day:

  Hello, Yoran, hey, hey. (4X)

  You have a green-and-yellow-striped shirt on. (3X)

  It's so good to see you here today.

Little Johnny Brown

African-American Folk Song | Adapted by Nina Araújo | CD Track 10
Song Card Page 98

Gm   D7   Gm
Little Johnny Brown, lay your blanket down.

         Cm D7   Gm
Little Johnny Brown, lay your blanket down.

Gm
Let's [say] [good-bye] to Seléne Motron.

Let's [wave] [good-bye] to Paddy Clancy.

Let's [bow] [good-bye] to Yeh-Eun Kyung.

Let's [say] [good-bye] to Johnny Brown.

Using the Song

Sing this song at the end of the day, and ask children to hold hands and walk around the circle as you say your good-byes to everyone. Having a circle at the end of the day reaffirms the sense of community that you build with children. Start with one child, and indicate which direction you will progress (clockwise or counterclockwise around the circle) so that everyone can predict which name will be sung next. If you are left with some verses after singing good-bye to all in the room, simply repeat, "Let's say good-bye to everyone" until the end, or if your next stop is the classroom door, "Let's walk together to our classroom door."

Variations

- This circle dance and game has been passed down through generations of African Americans living on the islands off the coast of South Carolina and Georgia. Some of the movements include folding blankets, choosing partners, and creating movements that partners imitate. Use this song in its original form as a game during waiting times. Elicit help from your children for the movement parts (for example, "What could we use for 'fold down a corner,' Rati?"):

  Little Johnny Brown, lay your blanket down. (2X)
  Oh! Fold down a corner, Johnny Brown.
  Fold another corner, Johnny Brown. (3X)
  Little Johnny Brown, lay your blanket down. (2X)
  Oh! Jump like a kangaroo, Johnny Brown. (4X)

Gatherings and Dismissals

Free choice time has ended, and the children in Susannah's classroom have almost finished putting materials away. She has planned to start a name game to invite children to the rug, where she is waiting to start a whole group gathering. She also uses this opportunity to send some children to use the restroom while she starts singing "Baked a Cake" (CD track 12). The children listen for a chance to join in by adding their own names and their favorite food. Susannah knows that this is also a great way to encourage social experiences through listening, taking turns, and encouraging awareness of others while building community in her classroom.

She invites children to participate and makes this transition smooth and appealing to them by understanding that not all of them need to join her at once. She realizes that waiting is not developmentally appropriate and prefers to gradually shift their attention at a pace appropriate to their age. She gently reminds them that they will gather for a little bit before the next activity, and she waits until they are all together in one group.

After her gathering time is over, the children in Susannah's classroom are hungry, and she decides to use a short chant to transition them to snack time before they all go outside to play. She starts the chant by telling her children that when they hear their names, they can stand up, wash their hands, and choose a seat to eat their snacks. Every day she ends the meeting with a chant or song, and today she chooses "Purple Stew" (CD track 17). Each child is familiar with the routine and chooses a stew flavor, happily leaving the meeting. Susannah always shares control of the day with the children in her class: she empowers them to make choices and actively participate in the process of transitioning from one activity to another during the day. This and many other planned transitions help the children change focus very smoothly. She keeps things predictable and familiar by using the same strategy to dismiss the children from her morning gathering meetings.

The More We Get Together

Traditional | Adapted by Nina Araújo | CD Track 11 | Song Card Page 99

    A   E   A
Oh! The more we get together, together, together.

                          E   A
Oh! The more we get together, the happier we'll be.

    E   A   E   A
There's [Tanya and Eric], and [Emma and LaKisha].

    A   E   A
Oh! The more we get together, the happier we'll be.

Using the Song

This song adds to the feeling of classroom community, as it includes all the children by using their names, and the emphasis on the word "together" creates a group feeling. Start singing this song as you gather children for a group meeting, and be sure to mention those who are not present. By acknowledging their absence, you maintain the connection so important for building communities. Let children take turns singing their friends' names. To inspire participation, start singing the song by including classroom pets' names, traveling stuffed animals, things from your daily planning (for example, playdough, water table, paints, easel, climber, books), etc. This way, you will give some children enough time to finish what they are doing so that they hear the group singing their names.

Variations

- Learn the ASL (American Sign Language) alphabet, and sign children's names individually.
- Put your arm around a neighbor and sway your bodies side to side to sing this song.
- This song can also be sung at the end of the day when saying good-bye:

  Oh! The more we get together, the happier we'll be.

  We'll say bye to Tanya, to Eric and Sylvio.

  Oh! The more we get together, the happier we'll be.

Baked a Cake

Traditional | Adapted by Carol Aghayan | CD Track 12 | Song Card Page 99

     A

If I knew [you] were coming, I'd have [baked a cake],

  E   A

[Baked a cake], [baked a cake].

                     A7

If I knew [you] were coming, I'd have [baked a cake].

      D   E   A

How-ja-doo, How-ja-doo, How-ja-doo.

     A

If I knew you were coming, I would [jump up and down],

  E   A

[Jump up and down], [jump up and down].

                     A7

If I knew you were coming, I would [jump up and down].

      D   E   A

How-ja-doo, How-ja-doo, How-ja-doo.

Using the Song

Ask individual children what they would like to bake; then try the opposite: "What would you like me to do if I knew you were coming to my house, Catara?" Incorporate their answers into the song. Ask children to demonstrate their ideas with their bodies (for example, "I would make some ice cream"—mimic eating the ice cream, etc.). Encourage all the children to imitate the motions chosen by each of their friends. Remember to document children's ideas on your song card so you can use them again later.

Variations

■ Sing the song with a friend's name, and try to ask for answers: ("If we knew Jake was coming we would . . ." "What could we do for you, Jake? What do you think, everyone?"). When you elicit help from the children in this song, you are inviting them to be an important part of your community as they learn to respect one another's ideas. They grow in confidence and learn about taking turns, listening, and diversity.

Everybody Shake a Hand

CD Track 13 | Song Card Page 99

(Tune: "Buffalo Gals")

A E7
Everybody [shake a hand], [shake a hand, shake a hand].
A D E7 A
Everybody [shake a hand], and [walk] around the room.
A E7
Everybody [give high five], [give high five, give high five].
A D E7 A
Everybody [give high five], and [walk] around the room.
A E7
Everybody [hug a friend], [hug a friend, hug a friend].
A D E7 A
Everybody [hug a friend], and [walk] around the room.

Using the Song

When children first try this song, some may struggle a bit with finding a partner and collaborating on the motions. With continuous practice and positive guidance, the process will get easier and more comfortable. Some children are more reserved about reaching out and finding a partner; some might just want to watch at first. Accept all forms of participation from your children. You can start chanting or whispering before adding the melody to the whole song. When the words and music are familiar to your children, they will enjoy walking or dancing around and greeting peers as they sing this song. Make up new motions and invite all children to do the same. When most children are focused on you, use this moment to transition them into the next activity ("Everybody sit like Anna, and curl down like a ball").

Variations

- If you have young children who are not interested in or are not yet ready for cooperative play, first give them an opportunity to use motions that don't require interactions with their peers, such as crawling like a bug, flying like a bird, swimming like a fish, etc. Gradually challenge them to use movements that help them connect with others, each in his or her own time.
- After you become used to the movement "walk around the room," ask your children for other ways to move around the room and incorporate their ideas into the song (for example, "and dance around the room").
- Sing this song, and ask children to greet one another when you sing their names:
  Everybody greet [Manuel], greet [Sophia], greet [Aidan].
  Everybody [greet] [Eliana], and [dance] around the room.

Lyrics by Jean Feldman. Reprinted with permission.

Gatherings and Dismissals

Stella Ella Olla

Traditional | CD Track 14 | Song Card Page 99

C
[Stella] [Ella] Olla,

Clap, clap, clap,

Singing esteega teega,

G7   C
Teega, teega, shack, shack.

C
Esteega, teega, valo, valo,

C
Valo, valo, valo va,

C
One, two, three, four, five!

Using the Song

This nonsense song is often popular among young children. Use it to gather children or while you wait for all the children to join you. With very young children, sing and gently tap their knees while singing to each child using a clap-slap pattern (for example, clap your hands and gently slap their knees). If you have older preschoolers, ask them to extend their hands, palms facing up. Each child puts the right hand over the hand of the child on the right and the left hand under the hand of the person on the left. You start by clapping your neighbor's right hand (which is on your left hand) with your right hand, and invite children to move the claps clockwise around the circle. Use the counting part at the end to cumulatively count the number of children who are present, who have had a chance to start the clapping, or whose name has been used once during this song ("Michael, Ichael, Olla"; "Eliza, Liza, Olla").

Variations

- Try using elbows that "click" each other and travel around the circle.
- Play with the sounds in this song. Sing something else for "shack, shack," or simply change the initial sound ("back, back"; "Jack, Jack"; etc.).

Over in the Meadow

Traditional | Adapted by Nina Araújo | CD Track 15 | Song Card Page 99

E
Over [in the meadow], [in the sand, in the sun]

      A   E   B7   E
Lived a friend named [Sônia] and a friend named [Clara].

 E   E7
[Dance], said Sônia. [I'll dance!], said [Clara].

        A   E   B7   E
And they [danced] and they [danced] [in the sand, in the sun].

Using the Song

Encourage the children to share their family way of greeting others, and incorporate this information into the song. Adapt the words to fit your geographical area and landscape features familiar to your children (for example, "Over at the beach, in the sand, in the sun"; "Down in the bayou, in the swamp, in the sun"). Remember to ask the first child whose name you sing what can be incorporated into the song. The information will guide the second child to join the first and follow the suggestion.

Variations

- Use the name of your school or classroom instead of geographical area (for example, "Over at the Children's Preschool")
- To add information, also include the unfamiliar or absurd (for example, "Over in the desert, in the snow, in the rain.")
- Use this song during good-bye transitions, and slightly adapt the words to include end-of-the-day rituals:

  Over [in the meadow], [in the sand, in the sun]

  Lived a friend named [Sônia] and a friend named [Clara].

  [Jump], said Sônia. [I'll jump!], said [Clara].

  And they [jumped] and [said] [good-bye] [in the sand, in the sun].

Gatherings and Dismissals

Bakery Shop

Traditional | CD Track 16 | Song Card Page 99

[Five] little [donuts] in the bakery shop

Looking so yummy with the [sprinkles] on the top.

Along came [Dylan] with a [penny] to pay.

He got this [donut], and he [walked] away.

Using the Song

Before you use this chant, remind children that when they hear their names, they can transition into the next activity. For example, if you are sending children to have snack, remind them that when they get their pretend donuts, they need to wash their hands, find a place to sit, etc. Start by asking the children to help you figure out how many donuts you will need in the chant according to the number of friends they have in class that day. This chant is great for including children and eliciting immediate participation from them. If donuts are not a word that is known or acceptable in your community, plan to start this chant with something familiar to your group (for example, muffins, bagels, etc.).

Variations

- Use a clap-slap pattern to help keep children focused (for example, thighs-hands, thighs-hands).
- Ask children to add their favorite topping to the donut, and personalize the chant by incorporating this information into the words.
- To add a bit of suspense and encourage children to recognize their written names, use name cards that can be bound and put on a ring. Show the name cards when you start chanting the third line so children can read their names along with you. For younger children, have their pictures on their name cards. Hang them anywhere in your classroom that is easily accessible to you and the children. They can help dismiss their friends and transition them into the next activity.

Purple Stew

Camp Song | CD Track 17 | Song Card Page 99

Making a [purple] [stew]. Making a [purple] [stubeedoobeedoo].

[Purple potatoes, and purple tomatoes]

And [Logan] in the purple stew! (point finger at chosen children when you say their names)

Using the Song

This camp chant offers many ways to keep children's attention on what is coming up next. Use this short rhyme to quickly dismiss children to transition into your next activity. Keep the chant exciting by closing your eyes and pointing with surprise at each child as you say "YOU in the purple stew."

   If your next activity is lunch, you can plan to use this chant to announce the menu for the day, if you are required to serve lunch, or to ask each child for one edible item that they have in their lunch boxes:

   Making a [sandwich] [stew]. Making a [yogurt] [stew]. Making a [string cheese] [stew].

   Making a [blueberry] [stew]. Making a [cookie] [stew]. Making a [juice] [stew].

   Making a [rice] [stew].

Variations

- Use this chant during waiting transitions as well.
- Help children take turns to dismiss their friends.
- Call out each child's name instead of "you" in the fifth line.
- Ask for what color potatoes and tomatoes you should have in the stew.
- Personalize this chant by titling the stew with individual children's names and dismissing three children at a time:

   Making an Eileen stew. Making a Jamby stubeedoobeedoo.

   Purple potatoes, and purple tomatoes, and Kolya in the purple stew!
- Use other types of cooked or baked plates in place of stew ("Making a purple quiche," "Making an orange pie," etc.).
- Play with many different sounds when you chant line 2. Add or completely change the "stubeedoobeedoo" part, and have fun taking risks with familiar and foreign sounds ("Making a burble boo, making a burble boobadeedodeedoo"; "Making a durkle doo, making a durkle dooda dee doo").
- After you are comfortable with this chant, try to add challenging clap-slap patterns, such as thigh-clap-snap, clap-clap-chest, etc. Or simply ask the children how they could keep the beat for this chant.

Gatherings and Dismissals

The Train Is a'Leaving

African-American Spiritual | Adapted by Nina Araújo | CD Track 18 | Song Card Page 99

      G

[The train] is a'leaving, oh yes. [The train] is a'leaving, oh yes.

              C

[Train] is a'leaving, [train] is a'leaving,

  G

[Train] is a'leaving, oh yes. Better get your tickets, oh yes. [Luc] get your tickets, oh yes.

                C

[André] get your tickets, [Pedrinho] get your tickets,

 C   G

[Vitor] get your tickets, oh yes.

Using the Song

All aboard! Everyone needs to get on the train to transition into the next activity. Trains fascinate young children, and so do other modes of transportation. The message is clear, and it helps you to keep your children focused on the upcoming change. Plan on creating a story that incorporates this train (or boat, or gondola, or bike), like telling children that, for example, the "snack train" is leaving and everyone needs to have tickets handy for when they hear their names being sung.

Variations

- Ask the children to take different roles or train cars to participate in the song:

  Who will be the conductor? oh yes. [children might volunteer right away]

  Jeff will be the conductor, oh yes.

  Jeff will be the conductor, Jeff will be the conductor.

  Jeff will be the conductor, oh yes.

- You can also use this song at the end of the day, when children are going home and you are saying good-bye to them as the caregiver shows up at the door, the bus line starts leaving, etc.

I Wonder What Tina Can Do

Traditional | Adapted by Nina Araújo | CD Track 19 | Song Card Page 99

```
    E              A         B7              E
I wonder, I wonder, I wonder what [Tina] can possibly do.

    E     E7       A         B7              E
I wonder, I wonder, I wonder what [Tina] can possibly do.

       E                        A
[She] can [play with blocks] or [paint at the easel]

    B7                   E
Or maybe [play with some glue].

    E     E7       A         B7              E
I wonder, I wonder, I wonder what [Tina] can possibly do.
```

Using the Song

When you sing this song, pretend to be puzzled to inspire your children to tell you what they will actually choose to do after you dismiss them. If they tell you something that you haven't mentioned in the song, act surprised!

Variations

- Invite your children to sing the refrain with you by singing, "We wonder what Tina can do."
- Try to sing this song at the end of the day as well, and modify the words to fit that transition:

    I wonder, I wonder, I wonder

    Where [Tina] can possibly go.

    I wonder, I wonder, I wonder

    Where [Tina] can possibly go.

    [She] might [go to the store] or [visit the dentist]

    Or maybe [she might go home].

    I wonder, I wonder, I wonder

    Where Tina can possibly go.

- If you have time, ask older preschoolers to give their peers clues about which activity they will do next, so that they can try to guess what their friend's choice is. Sing this song until you get to the line before last, and pause to find out where each child will go next. Incorporate the information into the modified last line of this song:

    I wonder, I wonder, I wonder

    Oh! Tina will play with some glue!

New Shoes, Old Shoes

Traditional | Adapted by Nina Araújo | CD Track 20 | Song Card Page 99

E
[New] [shoes], [old] [shoes]. [Zirque] has some [new] shoes.

A   B7   E
One, two, three, and four. Tap them gently on the floor.

E
[White] [shoes], [blue-striped] [shoes]. [Hanna] has some [white] shoes.

A   B7   E
One, two, three, and four. [Dance] them gently on the floor.

Using the Song

Sing this song during quick dismissals. You can personalize it by changing the words to describe each child's shoes (try to find something unique about each pair, and incorporate the details into the song). Prepare your children in advance by saying that when they find the shoes you are singing about on their feet, they may get up and start the next activity. To elicit direct participation from your children, sing "New shoes, old shoes, Adrián has some—" and stop at that point to give them a chance to notice their friend's shoes and to sing the answer. You can first ask the child you are singing about, to make sure you are using descriptors that are true for each child.

Variations

- To add something different, you can take only one shoe off the children's feet and put them all together in a bag or basket. Randomly select a shoe that needs its match, and indicate that when the owner is found, he or she will now transition into the next activity. Add the individual description to the song:

  [Pink] [shoes], [yellow] [shoes]. I have [Lisa's] [yellow] [shoes].

  One, two, three, and four. Tap them gently on the floor.

  [Put them on and walk to the door].

  (Add the last line if you're dismissing children to go somewhere with you.)

- Use different clothing items or parts of the body that children can use to tap the floor. Ask them what they want to tap, or clap, or shake every time you sing this song to dismiss them into the subsequent activity:

  Open hands, closed hands.

  Kyla has two open hands.

  One, two, three, and four.

  Clap them gently, here's some more!

Calling Attention

The children in Ms. Wiza's classroom go on a field trip to the local train station. When it's time to leave, Ms. Wiza wants to talk about some safety reminders before they exit the station. She needs all of the children's eyes and ears paying attention to her at that moment. She then starts singing "Do as I'm Doing" (CD track 21). All the children look at her to hear what she has to say. When they arrive back at the school, Ms. Wiza gathers them for a group meeting. The children haven't had a chance to use the restrooms and seem a bit restless. Ms. Wiza starts reading a book about the history of the train station they have just visited. Her children are less interested in what she is reading about than they were in the train station. She has to use three attention callers during a fifteen-minute group meeting before dismissing them to go outside to play.

Sometimes teachers realize that they have been using attention callers more often than they would like to. The need to call children's attention may be an indication that we should modify the way we plan for group times. Perhaps they are too long or don't hold the children's interest. Maybe they are not age appropriate, or maybe we have not adequately included children during those times. Sometimes our schedules don't have a balanced combination of active and quiet play. The key here is to use these attention callers as a strategy for redirecting attention but also as a tool for evaluation of our programming.

Do as I'm Doing

Traditional | Adapted by Carol Aghayan | CD Track 21 | Song Card Page 100

A
Do as [I'm] doing,

              E
Follow, follow [me].

A
Do as [I'm] doing,

E7   A
Follow, follow [me].

A
Do as [Susie's] doing,

              E
Follow, follow [her].

A
Do as [Susie's] doing,

E7   A
Follow, follow [her].

A
Sit as [I'm] sitting,

              E
Follow, follow [me].

A
Sit as [I'm] sitting,

E7   A
Follow, follow [me].

Using the Song

This song is a variation of the popular American game "Simon Says." Start by focusing on what you are doing, to attract attention from everyone in your classroom. After that, call attention to what individual children are doing, and invite the other children to join in. End this song with "quiet lines," such as "Sit as Bernadette is sitting, follow, follow her"; or "Shh as I am shhing, follow, follow me." Sing the first two lines; then hum the last two. Use this song during gathering transitions as well. End the song with a clapping pattern without words as you redirect their focus and energy level to start the next activity (for example, clap-slap-clap-slap in the rhythm to the chant).

A Ram Sam Sam

Traditional | Adapted by Nina Araújo | CD Track 22 | Song Card Page 100

   A
A ram sam sam. (slap your thighs) A ram sam sam. (slap your thighs)

   D
Guli guli guli guli guli. (roll your hands over each other)

   A
Ram sam sam. (slap your thighs)

[Arafi], [arafi]. (raise your arms high and bring them down low)

   E
Guli guli guli guli guli. (roll your hands over each other)

  A
Ram sam sam. (slap your thighs)

  A
Stop, look, and listen. Stop, look, and listen.

   D
Guli guli guli guli guli.

 A
Stop, look, and listen. [Arafi], [arafi].

   E
Guli guli guli guli guli.

 A
Stop, look, and listen.

Using the Song

Use this nonsense song to redirect children's attention to you. If, after you have sung it a few times, some children haven't noticed what's going on, substitute their names for "Arafi."

If you typically use a spoken "stop, look, and listen" approach, include these words in the song as you change from your talking voice to your singing voice to call children's attention (as demonstrated on the companion CD).

Open and Shut Them

Traditional | CD Track 23 | Song Card Page 100

A
Open and shut them, open and shut them, (open and close hands)

         E
Give a little [clap, clap, clap]. (clap hands as you sing "clap, clap, clap")

A
Open and shut them, open and shut them (open and close hands)

D   E   A
Lay them in your lap, lap, lap. (tap lap as you sing "lap, lap, lap")

       A
[Creep] them, [crawl] them, [creep] them, [crawl] them (fingers crawl to your chin)

           E
Right up to your chin, chin, chin. (tap chin as you sing "chin, chin, chin")

A   A7
Open up your little mouth (open your mouth and slowly crawl fingers around it)

    D   E   A
But do not let them in! (said hurriedly) (hide hands behind your back)

Using the Song

This song is especially effective with very young children and can be used for many different transitions, although it seems to work best to call attention. Vary the volume (louder and softer) and tempo (mixing slower and faster over the course of the song) to engage the children. Change the way your fingers reach your chin to fully capture their attention (for example, "fly them, glide them"; "jump them, skip them").

Calling Attention

Put Your Finger on Your Nose

Traditional | Adapted by Carol Aghayan | CD Track 24 | Song Card Page 100

(The first six lines of this song are chanted.)

Put your finger on your nose.

And put your finger on your toes.

Put your finger on your lips.

And put your finger on your hips.

Put your finger on your knees.

Hands in your lap now, please.

A   E A
Put your finger on your nose, on your toes, on your lips.

       E   A
Put your finger on your knees. Hands in your lap now, please.

  A   E
Put your finger on your nose.

  E7   A
Put your finger on your toes.

  A   E
Put your finger on your lips.

  E7   A
Put your fingers on your hips.

  A7   D
Put your fingers on your knees.

   A E A
Hands in your lap now, please.

Using the Song

This rhyme can be used with a familiar melody, such as "London Bridge" or "Happy Birthday"; with a made-up melody; or as a chant. Act out the song in an exaggerated way to invite the children to do the same and focus on you. Make purposeful mistakes to encourage them to pay attention and as a way to add humor to the song (for example, sing "Put your finger on your nose," but then put your finger on your shoulder instead).

Sit on Your Bottom

CD Track 25 | Song Card Page 100

CD Track 25 | Song Card Page 100

```
 A                    D       E
[Sit on your bottom] now just for me.

 A            D        E
I love [you], and [you] love me.

    A                   D          E
That way we'll all be as happy as can be

       E7          A
By the time I count to one-two-three.

One, two, three.

   A                 D      E
[Hands to yourself] now just for me.

 A            D        E
I love [you], and [you] love me.

    A                 D         E
That way we'll all be as happy as can be

       E7          A
By the time I count to one-two-three.

One, two, three.
```

Using the Song

This song sends a clear message to the children. It has short lines and quick reminders of what they need to do to redirect their attention to what you need to say. It can be very effective when used in the middle of whole group gatherings to help the children re-center and focus on what's happening. You can also share the lead in this song by asking the children to "surprise" you. You close your eyes and only open them when they are ready to hear what you have to say ("I wonder if you will be sitting down when I open my eyes. Oh, I know you will!"). Use the first line to remind your children of what they need to focus on ("Pick up the toys now just for me"; "Stand in the line now just for me"). In line 2, include children's names to add encouragement.

Lyrics by Margaret Sansovich. Reprinted with permission.

Calling Attention

Only One Can Talk at a Time

CD Track 26 | Song Card Page 100

A
Only one can talk at a time

And this is what I'll do,

I'll sit as still as a little mouse

    E   A
Until other folks are through.

Using the Song

This song reminds children of a basic social rule for group care: only one person talks at a time. While that person is speaking, others are listening and waiting for a turn to talk. Children like to imitate animals, and the invitation to imitate a small mouse calls their attention to this important rule in a playful and developmentally appropriate way. It also helps to sing line 3 in a quiet voice to imitate the "quiet" mouse.

Lyrics by Jean Feldman. Reprinted with permission.

A Little Bit Up

Unknown Source | CD Track 27 | Song Card Page 100

    A   D

A little bit up (arms go up high), and a little bit down. (arms go down low)

    E   A

A little bit up (arms go up high), and a little bit down. (arms go down low)

                          A7   D

A little bit up (arms go up high), and a little bit down. (arms go down low)

    E   E7   A

That's what makes the world go around. (turn around in place)

                                  E

I have two hands; I'm gonna make them move. (move hands freely)

                                A

I have two hands; I'm gonna make them move. (move hands freely)

                         D

I have two hands; I'm gonna make them move. (move hands freely)

    E   E7   A

That's what makes the world go around. (turn around in place)

                                E

I have two feet; I'm gonna make them move. (move feet freely)

                                A

I have two feet; I'm gonna make them move. (move feet freely)

                         D

I have two feet; I'm gonna make them move. (move feet freely)

    E   E7   A

That's what makes the world go around. (turn around in place)

Using the Song

When you need to redirect your children in the middle of a busy or rainy day, this song is for you! Its whole-body movements and opportunities for participation fully engage the children. Take the time to listen to how children want to move and stretch their bodies before they need to be quiet to hear what you have to say; it will help them be more attentive. You can change the energy level by whispering the song and changing the last line to "That's what makes everybody sit down," followed by quiet body movements like "I've got two sighs; I'm gonna make them sound."

Five Little Hotdogs

Traditional | CD Track 28 | Song Card Page 100

Five little hotdogs frying in the pan. (five fingers facing down on facing up palm)

The pan got hot

And one went (rub fingers on palm pretending it is the pan)

BAM! (end with a huge clap and a loud BAM!)

(Continue with "Four little hotdogs . . . ," etc., until the last hotdog goes BAM!)

Using the Song

This chant has contrasting verses that are very good for calling children's attention, and it works best when you need to remind children of safety rules before and after field trips, nature walks, etc. Many children find it difficult to shift quickly from active play to quiet mode to hear what you have to say, and this song allows them to release their energy before focusing on the task at hand. Encourage children to be really loud at "BAM!" This will keep them focused as they look forward to that final loud moment. At the end of the chant, when there are no more hotdogs left, change the words slightly to change energy levels before you need their full attention on you:

> No little hotdogs frying in the pan.
> The pan cooled off and . . .

If you have children who are uncomfortable with loud noises, find a volume level that is good for all children in the room without singling out those who don't like noisy songs.

Five Little Peas

Traditional | CD Track 29 | Song Card Page 100

[Five little peas] in a [pea pod] pressed. (cup two hands and pretend there are peas hidden inside them)

One grew, two grew, (separate your hands from each other but not completely)

And so did the rest.

They grew and grew and did not stop, (inflate your hands until they look like a ball)

Until one day they all went [POP]! (clap hands and invite children to do the same)

Using the Song

This short chant helps focus children's attention on what's inside your hands. The combination of suspense and anticipation of the loud "pop!" helps you hold their attention until you have all children gathered around you to hear what you have to say. You might have to chant it more than once; for the last time, if your children are not yet sitting down, you can change the "pop" for "flop" and act out the flopping until you reach the floor while inviting them to do the same. Be silly, and change the words to make this chant more meaningful to them, if necessary:

Eighteen children in a child pod pressed . . .

Before you use this version, you can capture their attention by pretending that you are putting each child inside the "child pod" by saying each child's name and, with your fingers, pointing to the children inside your hands to make sure that they're all there.

Two Little Houses

Traditional | CD Track 30 | Song Card Page 100

Two little [houses] closed up tight. (give one big clap)

Let's open the [windows] and let in some light. (separate your hands and stretch your fingers wide, pretending they are windows)

[Ten] little finger people tall and straight. (point at each child to make sure they know to whom you are talking)

Ready to sit down by the time I count to eight! (count to eight and invite them to sit down)

Using the Song

Counting chants often help children focus on what is going to happen when a certain number is reached. To make this fun, cover your eyes while you are counting to eight, and demonstrate surprise when your children tell you that it's okay to open them. Substitute everyday words for "house" to reflect your community or the children's living situations (two little huts, two little apartments, two little flats, two little houseboats, etc.). Do the same with "windows" (doors, screens, cat door, etc.). Incorporate your children's home languages in the counting.

Cleaning Up

Fifteen minutes before the next activity, Mr. Morales walks around his class-room with a puppet he uses exclusively at clean-up time (it only "wakes up" at this time of day!), letting the children know that they have five minutes to play before it is time to clean up the room. The children have just enjoyed one hour of free play time. There is a lot of work to do, so Mr. Morales starts cleaning up some areas as he gently reminds the children that time will be up soon. He starts singing "Cleaning Spirit" (CD track 37) as he and the children pick up the toys and put them away. Soon most of them are asking for a job in the classroom, and the whole group is ready to start the next activity.

Cleaning up the classroom is a necessity, and it can be one of the most chal-lenging transitions for teachers and children alike. It can be stressful because for many children the concept of "cleaning up" is rather broad and often means "dumping out" or picking up one item during the whole transition. To minimize confusion among the children, Mr. Morales uses a nonverbal warning signal before he really needs to start cleaning up the room (and not just five minutes before the next activity!). Mr. Morales has repeatedly used his "clean-up puppet" as a warning signal until it's become familiar to the children and adults in the room. He models teamwork as he clears some areas in the room, inviting them to join in. Likewise, he has been using the same song (with interesting and amusing variations, of course!) during clean-up time for several months already; the chil-dren know what to expect while they sing along, making this transition a fun one. He uses different rhythms, chants it sometimes, and incorporates American Sign Language from time to time, as his puppet cannot hear with its ears.

How About You?

Traditional | CD Track 31 | Song Card Page 101
(Tune: "Skip to My Lou")

A
[I] can [put the books away]; how about you?

E
[I] can [put the books away]; how about you?

A   A7
[I] can [put the books away]; how about you?

  D   E7   A
How about you, [my darling]?

 A
[Erin] can [help pick up blocks]; how about you?

E
[Erin] can [help pick up blocks]; how about you?

A   A7
[Erin] can [help pick up blocks]; how about you?

  D   E7   A
How about you, [dear Brian]?

 A
[Brian] [picks the puzzles up]; how about you?

 E
[Brian] [picks the puzzles up]; how about you?

 A   A7
[Brian] [picks the puzzles up]; how about you?

  D   E7   A
How about [my friend Madeline]?

Using the Song

Use a warning signal that prepares your children for the upcoming change of activities, and start singing this song while modeling desirable behaviors (start picking things up off the floor and put them away). Make sure that they can see what you are doing (for example, clean off a shelf in the room at the children's eye level).

Start a new verse that follows a spoken question with a child's name ("How about you, Sienna? What can you do, Sienna?"). This encourages children to notice and recognize participation and teamwork efforts, big or small. Children become involved at clean-up time at different

How About You? (continued)

paces. Be mindful of this variation, and encourage children by replacing "How about my friend [name]?" with "Thank you so much, dear [name]!" the final time through the song.

Incorporate clean-up tasks into the song that you can see in progress while you are singing (for example, "Analee can put books away; how about you?"). The emphasis here should be on invitation rather than competition.

If you have a child in your room who cannot move easily or cannot see very well, find a way to include him or her in this transition. Emphasize how important it is to have that child's help by adding his or her tasks to the song (for example, "Hunter can watch the trash can; how about you?"—Hunter is in a wheelchair and can remind friends to pick up trash off the floor; "Elise can wash the tables"—Elise is blind).

Variations

- If you don't want to interrupt the singing, especially when the children are cooperating and engaged, you can substitute the spoken question with a sung version:

  How about you, Sienna, how can you help?

  How about you, Sienna, how can you help?

  How about you, Sienna, how can you help?

  How can you help, my darling?

- If you see two children in one area, you can include both of them in your song ("How can you help, Chris and Ahmed?").

We're Gonna Clean

Traditional | Adapted by Nina Araújo | CD Track 32 | Song Card Page 101
(Tune: "You Gotta Sing")

             Em   B7   Em
[We're] gonna [clean] when the [spirit] says [clean].

             Em   B7   Em
[We're] gonna [clean] when the [spirit] says [clean].

          C
When the [spirit] says [clean]

          Em
[We're] gonna [clean] right along.

               B7   Em
[We're] gonna [clean] when the [spirit] says [clean].

Using the Song

Sing this song wholeheartedly, as Ruth Seeger says! You can also create a weekly job for this part of the day—a "clean-up-time reminder" who will walk around the room and help other children with incomplete jobs.

Variations

- Change the words to include specific clean-up jobs:

   We're gonna put away [the toys] when we're done.

   We're gonna put away [the toys] when we're done.

   When we're done with [the toys]

   We're gonna put them away.

   We're gonna put away [the toys] when we're done.

- Change the style of the song, and make it fun and different while keeping the same words: sing to opera, rap, chant, while keeping the expectations for this transition clear.

- Adapt the words to fit your cultural context ("pick up," "clean up," "tidy up," "save the toys").

- This song can also be used during waiting times if you ask children what they would like to do when someone tells them to (for example, "We're gonna jump when Alyia says jump").

I Like the Way

Traditional | CD Track 33 | Song Card Page 101

A   E
I like the way that [Shawanda] is cleaning up and [Jessica] is cleaning up

    A
And [Ana] is cleaning up.

                       A7
I like the way that [Andrew] is cleaning up

D   E7   A
On this [Tuesday] morning.

A   E
I like the way that [Shamika] is cleaning up and [Dylan] is cleaning up

    A
And [Christopher] is cleaning up.

                       A7
I like the way that [Monique] is cleaning up

D   E7   A
On this [Tuesday] morning.

Using the Song

Sing this song to encourage teamwork by making sure that you include everyone's names in it. Avoid singing about one single child and not following through with all the other children. Use several children's names throughout each repetition of the song to encourage participation and discourage competition. Recognize everyone's efforts to participate in this transition by describing what individual children are doing.

Variations

- Replace "On this [day of the week] morning" with "Thank you so much, Tierry" to thank children for their hard work (or "Thank you so much my friends!").
- This song can be sung throughout the day to appropriately praise children for acceptable and positive behaviors ("I like the way that Hesaki is washing his hands"; "I like the way that Sônia uses gentle touches," etc.).
- Use ongoing clean-up tasks as you spot them (for example, "I like the way that Ashley is putting blocks away"; or "I like the way that Hesaki is emptying the water table").

Blocks Go to Sleep

Unknown Source | CD Track 34 | Song Card Page 101

G   G7
[Blocks] go to sleep [on the shelf, on the shelf]. Hurry, [Luc], and put them over there.

      C   Am   G   Em
Let's clean up, pick up, help our friend [Oliver].

   G   D   G
[Blocks] go to sleep [on the shelf, on the shelf].

   G   G7
[Paintbrushes] go to sleep [in the sink, in the sink]. Hurry, [André], and put them over there.

      C   Am   G   Em
Let's clean up, pick up, help our friend [Chris].

   G   D   G
[Paintbrushes] go to sleep [in the sink, in the sink].

Using the Song

Young children can empathize with the idea of resting after busy times; they might rest at nap-time in a full-day program, and they go to sleep at night at the end of a busy school day. They often seem to enjoy singing about objects that "go to sleep" as they do, and this song can help them to "separate" from toys and develop trust that they will "wake up" again soon. Plan to ask individual children where they think that certain toys live or sleep, and include this information in the song ("Home toys go to sleep in the cubby, in the cubby").

Variations

- Adapt this song according to the design and configuration of your classroom.
- You can elicit help from your children by singing a question and using a short pause for their answers.

  Where do markers sleep, dear Ian, dear Ian?

  Pause to listen to Ian's answer.

  Hurry then and put them over there. Let's clean up, pick up, help our friend Anna.

  Markers go to sleep on the shelf, on the shelf.

- If you are singing about a last task, you can end the song by inviting children to start the next activity. For example, if you're starting a whole group meeting, sing:

  Scissors go to sleep in the basket, in the basket. Hurry, Terry, and put them over there.

  Let's clean up, finish up. Meet me on the rug.

  All the toys are sleeping, and our work is done!

Tidy Up

Adapted by Carol Aghayan | CD Track 35 | Song Card Page 101

(Tune: "Jingle Bells")

  A

Tidy up, tidy up, put the [toys] away.

  D   A   E7

Tidy up, tidy up, we're finished for today.

  A   A7

Tidy up, tidy up, put the [toys] away.

  D   A   E   E7   A

For we'll take them out again next time we come to play.

  A

Tidy up, tidy up, [Grace], put the [books] away.

  D   A   E7

Tidy up, tidy up we're finished for today.

  A   A7

Tidy up, tidy up, [André], put the [blocks] away.

  D   A   E   E7   A

For we'll take them out again next time we come to play.

Using the Song

This song can help children who struggle to separate from toys at clean-up time. Add verbal reminders to reinforce the last line in the song (for example: "See, Ana? The blocks will be waiting for you right here when you come back tomorrow"). It is important to be specific when you sing each child's name and match it with the clean-up job that he or she is doing.

Variations

- Not all clean-up jobs involve tidying up and putting things away. At this time, children can help with jobs like draining the water table, wiping the tables off, washing cooking materials, sweeping the floor—to name a few. Adapt this song to include a variety of jobs that happen simultaneously.

- If you want to be more specific and include more children at once, you can use this version of "Tidy Up":

  Pick up blocks, pick up pots, [Jennifer], put the [toys] away.

  Pick up markers, pick up dolls, we're finished for today.

  Pick up books, pick up brushes, [Cecilia], put the [toys] away.

  For we'll take them out again next time we come to play.

Lyrics by Jean Feldman. Reprinted with permission.

There Was an Old Friend

Traditional | Adapted by Nina Araújo | CD Track 36 | Song Card Page 101
(Tune: "There Was an Old Frog")

       G   D   G

There was an old friend, and [his] name was [Geraldo]. Ching-a chang-a polly mitch-a cow-me-o.

                                                  D   G

[He] came to play and put things away. Ching-a chang-a polly mitch-a cow-me-o.

[He] [put away blocks] and helped all around,

    C   G

Around and around until there was nothing sitting on the ground.

              D   G

Ching-a chang-a polly mitch-a cow-me-o.

Using the Song

Learn this song well before introducing it to your children. It has strange sounds that break the structure of the song to add a playful atmosphere to this transition, but they can be difficult to remember without practice. Describe the clean-up job that matches each child's name in line 5.

Variations

- You can just use sounds in lines 2 and 4 that are simpler to sing all the way through (for example, "There was an old friend, and his name was Gus, diddle diddle diddle diddle diddle dee-o").
- Try chanting it for a while before you sing it.
- After using this song for a while, leave lines 2 and 4 out, and let the children fill in the blanks.
- This song can be used during waiting times if you add body motions to be used with "Ching-a chang-a polly mitch-a cow-me-o."
- This song can also be used at the end of the day to say good-bye:

  There was an old friend, and [her] name was [Rita].

  Ching-a chang-a polly mitch-a cow-me-o.

  She liked going home to [play with her sister].

  Ching-a chang-a polly mitch-a cow-me-o.

  [She] said [tchau, tchau] and waved all around,

  Around and around until there was nobody sitting on the ground.

  Ching-a chang-a polly mitch-a cow-me-o.

Cleaning Spirit

Camp Song | Adapted by Nina Araújo | CD Track 37 | Song Card Page 101

A
[Anna] has that [clean-my-classroom] spirit,

Right in [her] [head], [she's] got it,

E
Right in [her] [head], [she's] got it,

A
Right in [her] [head].

[Anna] has that [clean-my-classroom] spirit,

             A7   D
Right in [her] [head], [she's] got it,

           E   A E A
Right in [her] [head] to sta-a-ay.

Using the Song

This song is especially appropriate for older preschoolers. Don't expect to see children singing along right away. Most children prefer to listen to it for a while first and then participate at certain times before singing the entire song. This is a great song to keep children focused on the goal for this transition while enjoying the playfulness of the actions and words.

Plan to use motions that highlight the different body parts or other words that your children add to the song (for example, Melina might say, "right in my house").

Variations

- Challenge children by singing "Who's got that clean-my-classroom spirit?" When a child volunteers, ask where he or she has it, and start the song again with that child's name.
- When you sing the last line, leave "stay" out so children can all sing it together.
- This song can also be used during any daily transition, like saying good-bye:

  I've got that [see you tomorrow] spirit

  or during waiting:

  I've got that [school's name] spirit.

What Can You Clean, Ponchinella Funny Fellow?

Traditional | Adapted by Carol Aghayan | CD Track 38 | Song Card Page 101

       A
What can you clean, Ponchinella funny fellow?

              E7   A
What can you clean, Ponchinella funny you?

[Luc] can [pick up puzzles], Ponchinella funny fellow.

              E7   A
[Luc] can [pick up puzzles], Ponchinella funny you.

[Kendrick] [cleans the brushes], Ponchinella funny fellow.

              E7   A
[Kendrick] [cleans the brushes], Ponchinella funny you.

What can you clean, Ponchinella funny fellow?

              E7   A
What can you clean, Ponchinella funny you?

Using the Song

Use this song when your children are learning to make choices. Point to a child when you sing "you" on the second line to make your selection clear. Listen for an answer, and incorporate it into the song.

Variations

- This song can be used differently with older preschoolers: children take turns pointing and choosing different friends to make clean-up job choices.
- This song can also be used during waiting times for fun. Children take turns being Ponchinella, choosing an action that others will imitate:

  (Children:) What can you do, Ponchinella funny fellow? What can you do, Ponchinella funny you?

  (Ponchinella:) I can swing around, Ponchinella funny fellow. I can swing around, Ponchinella funny you!

  (Other children, as they swing around like Ponchinella:) We can do this too, Ponchinella funny fellow. We can do this too, Ponchinella funny you!

Pick Up

Adapted by Carol Aghayan | CD Track 39 | Song Card Page 101
(Tune: "Jada")

```
   E      (C#m)   B7                    E
[Liani], [pick up, pick up] all the [toys] now.

   E      (C#m)   F#m                   B7
[Sienna], [pick up, pick up] all the [toys] now.

   E             B7      E
All day long we work and play.

   E             B7      E
Now it's time to put them away.

   E      (C#m)    A          B7    E
[Milan], [pick up, pick up] all the [toys] now.
```

Using the Song

Use two names at a time to encourage teamwork and collaboration among children. This song has a steady beat, and it especially helps children who have a higher activity level during this transition. Try to be specific with the clean-up job that children choose to take (lines 1, 2, and 5) to help them focus and have fun during this transition ("Ayda, Ayda, wash all the brushes now"; "Rati, Rati, put the books away now"). Toward the end, sing this song very slowly, while you change the activity level and gradually transition the children into the next activity.

Variations

▨ Leave some lines off, and let children fill in the blanks for you.

And We Hunted and We Found

Traditional | Adapted by Nina Araújo | CD Track 40 | Song Card Page 101
(Tune: "And We Hunted, and We Hunted")

          A
And we hunted, and we hunted, and we hunted, and we found

        D   E   A
Some [books] [on the floor]. And then we looked around–lookee there!

[Some] [say] there are some [blocks], and others say nay.

                                    D   E   A
[Some] [say] there are some [markers] that we need to put away–lookee there!

          A
And we hunted, and we hunted, and we hunted, and we found

        D   E   A
Some [crayons] [on the floor]. And then we looked around–lookee there!

[Chris] [says] there are some [pipe cleaners], and others say nay.

                                    D   E   A
[Alyia] [says] there are some [games] that we need to put away–lookee there!

Using the Song

Adapt this song to include familiar clean-up jobs. This song is especially appropriate to use with preschool-age children. Note the repetition of "and we hunted." Use this opportunity to invite children to keep looking for items that need to be cleaned up and to get involved in teamwork during this transition. This song offers an interesting approach to clean-up time: you ask children to look for things that need to be put away, and when they find them, they feel especially proud for having found what you could not. This is the perfect moment to invite the "finder" to put the item away. When you are singing the song, stop at "say" right before "nay," and let your children finish that line in the song.

Variations

- Sometimes start this transition by chanting this song to help children focus on what is happening at this time of day, and then change to singing mode.
- Sing the last verse a bit differently to let everyone know that cleanup is finished:
  And we hunted, and we hunted, and we hunted, and we found
  [Nothing] [on the floor]. And then we looked around–lookee there!
  [Chris] [says] there's [nothing left], and others say nay.
  [Alyia] [says] there's [nothing] that we need to put away–we are done!

Moving

Ms. Debbie and Ms. Joy are helping children get ready to go to the playground. Their school only has access to the outdoors through a long hallway. Ms. Debbie has plans to make this transition playful. As she sees them getting ready, she starts singing, "I've got a friend that you all know, and Ashley is her name! Get on board, little children, there's room for many a more!" (CD track 41). In this way she invites individual children to get on board. She also asks them to join her in packing invisible bags for this trip. She carefully reminds children that they can take turns being the conductor as they "travel" to the playground.

Seldom do we have the luxury of a classroom door that opens into the playground. It is in the best interest of the children that Ms. Debbie and Ms. Joy plan for this transition. Moving from one place to another can be challenging, even with a small group of children. Some moving transitions require children to be quiet, while others can be noisier. These teachers make the most of it by creating an adventure and setting the children up for success by having fun with them. They can incorporate all kinds of things that children can naturally add to the songs: marching, clapping, stomping, pretending they are quiet animals—the possibilities are endless. You cannot go wrong when you include children's imagination in your journey.

Get On Board, Little Children

CD Track 41 | Song Card Page 102

  A
I've got a friend that you all know

     E   A
And [Jacintha] is her name.

I've got a friend that you all know

     E   A
And [Maddy] is her name.

          A7
Get on board, [little children],

     D   A
Get on board, [little children],

          F#m
Get on board, [little children],

     E   E7   A
There's room for many a more.

I've got a friend that you all know

     E   A
And [Steven] is his name.

I've got a friend that you all know,

     E   A
And [Evelyn] is her name.

          A7
Get on board, [little Steven],

     D   A
Get on board, [little Evelyn],

          F#m
Get on board, [my friend Spencer],

     E   E7   A
There's room for many a more.

     E   E7   A
There's room for many a more.

Using the Song

Most children get excited about vehicles. Sing this song to role-play a trip somewhere using various modes of transportation (some more unusual choices: gondolas, bikes, trikes, chariots, ships, strollers, elephants, horses, donkeys, taxicabs, subways, monorails). This simple song can gather children from play areas to prepare to leave the room and go outside (or anywhere they need to go). Touch children on the shoulder to signal them to get on board as the vehicle moves from one place to another.

Variations

- Use children's names in place of "little children," and adapt the first portion of the song to describe the type of transportation you will use each time you sing this song. To add suspense, give children hints, and ask them to guess how you will arrive at your destination:

  I've got a car that you all know.

  Playground here we come . . .

  I've got a cab that you all know.

  Cafeteria, here we come . . .

  I've got a plane that you all know

  And library, here we come . . .

- Give children turns leading their friends or choosing the transportation they will take.
- Use two children's names at once when your time is limited ("Get on board, Kim and Zirque; get on board, Jean and Lucas").

Lyrics by Jean Feldman. Reprinted with permission.

We're on Our Way

Traditional | Adapted by Nina Araújo | CD Track 42 | Song Card Page 102

A
[We're] on our way, [we're] on our way,

       E7
On [our] way to [play outside].

[We're] on our way, [we're] on our way,

       A
On [our] way to [play outside].

          E E7 A
When [we] go outside, [we're] gonna [ride the trikes].

          E E7 A
When [we] go outside, [we're] gonna [ride the trikes].

         E
[Russell], [he rides the trikes] like this.

 E7   A
[Russell], [he rides the trikes] like this.

Using the Song

Start singing this song while the children are getting ready to go somewhere to help them antici-pate the next activity. The lyrics engage them in thinking about all the things they can do when they go outside. Sing the chorus many times as teachers and children move to the playground.

Variations

- Use words that are familiar to your routine, playground setting, or community.
- Elicit contributions from the children ("Who can think of something else that we can do outside?").
- Adapt this song to use it during other transitions ("We're on our way, on our way to eat some lunch"; "We're on our way, on our way to take the bus").

This Train Is Bound for Glory

Traditional | Adapted by Nina Araújo | CD Track 43 | Song Card Page 102

Am
This [train] is bound for [glory],

 G
[Olga] is bound for [glory],

 Am
[Ivan] is bound for [glory],

    C   E   Am
[Children] get on board.

Am
No more [painting and gluing],

G
No more [painting and gluing],

Am
No more [painting and gluing],

    C   E   Am
[Children] get on board.

Using the Song

Invite your children to be a train car (hopper car, caboose, freight car, flatbed car, coach car, restaurant car, etc.) or a special "name car" (for example, "Marisa car"). Walk around the room, and as you sing children's names, touch each child on the shoulder to signal him or her to "get on board." When it's time to return to the classroom, send an "All aboard!" call to help them "get on board" again. You will find that some children want to be boats or construction cars-simply adapt the lyrics to reflect their choices. In lines 6, 7, and 8, name the activities you were doing just before you had to leave as a reminder that you are doing something else now.

Variations

- Add your destination to the song (for example, "This gondola is bound for the play-ground," or "This digger is bound for our classroom").

Moving

Follow Me

Traditional | Adapted by Carol Aghayan | CD Track 44 | Song Card Page 102

Follow me, [Gábi], follow me.

Point to things that you can see.

Put your hand on top of your [head].

And point to something that is [red].

Using the Song

Use a slap-clap pattern to set a rhythm with this chant. If you need to call a child's attention, use his or her name between the two "follow me's" in line 1. This chant can also be used during waiting times.

Variations

- Change the slap-clap pattern, and encourage children to make up their own patterns as well.
- Use nonsense words that rhyme with a color or color pattern that you want children to look for (for example, "Put your hand on top of your 'crink,' and point to something that is pink").
- Use some absurd ideas to keep the rhyming pattern (for example, "Put your hand on top of your tray, and point to something that is gray").
- Here are some starting ideas:

    . . . shoe . . . blue.

    . . . back . . . black.

    . . . where you bite . . . white.

    Wave your hands to say hello . . . yellow.

    Wave your hands up and down . . . brown.

Jim Along Josie

Traditional | CD Track 45 | Song Card Page 102

A   E   A
Hey, [come along], Jim along Josie. Hey, [come along], Jim along Joe.

A   E   A
Hey, [hop along, hop along] [children]. Hey, [hop along, hop along] [friends].

A   E   A
Hey, [hop along, hop along] [Maddie]. Hey, [hop along, hop along] [Grace].

A   E   A
Hey, [tiptoe, tiptoe] [Layla]. Hey, [tiptoe, tiptoe] [Reghan].

A   E   A
Hey, [march along, march along] [friends]. Hey, [march along, march along] [friends].

A
Hey, [come sit down, come sit down] [boys and girls],

                              E   A
Hey, [come sit down, come sit down] [friends].

Using the Song

Tell children where you are heading, and elicit help from them by saying, "How can we move our bodies to get to the cafeteria today?" Create an atmosphere of acceptance by changing the song to include children's ideas. This will make them feel invited to participate and to join the group in moving somewhere. Use the song to gather children together after the journey if appropriate (for example, "Hey come sit down, come sit down everyone. Hey come sit down, come sit down friends"). Invite children by simply singing, "Hey, come along, come along, Josephine."

Variations

- Pair children up, and use both names with the same action ("Hey, hop along, hop along Mirella. Hey, hop along, hop along Susannah").
- To add fun, use a body motion to emphasize the "Hey" part of this song (big clap, stomp, clap up high, etc.).
- Hum all the words, and only sing each child's name. While you're humming, act out the movement that you would like the children to do together (flap your arms for "fly along," exaggerate your stomping to "stomp along," etc.).

Betty Martin

Traditional | Adapted by Nina Araújo | CD Track 46 | Song Card Page 102

```
 C                G7    C
Hey, [Betty Martin], [tiptoe, tiptoe],

 C7                   G     C
Hey, [Betty Martin], [tiptoe] fine.

 C            G7       C
Hey, [Analee], [walking, walking],

 C7            G      C
Hey, [Analee], [walking] fine.
```

Using the Song

Sing this song when traveling to nearby destinations. Using children's first and last names makes this song interesting and different; most children are not used to hearing each other's full names. But using only a first name works as well. You can also add your own full name to pique their curiosity, making yourself a part of the song. This song also helps children focus on acceptable moving behaviors rather than on things they cannot do.

Variations

- Shout the "Hey" part, and contrast it with soft singing for the rest of the song.
- After repeated use of this song, sing children's first names, and wait until your children fill in the blanks with the last names. The challenge will also help them focus on what is happening during the transition.
- Use this song to highlight acceptable behaviors that you notice during the day. This also works well as a gentle reminder of appropriate behaviors that are expected to be used in the classroom ("Hey, Adam Rozman, quiet, quiet, hey Adam Rozman, quiet now"; "Hey, Lekeitha, listen, listen, hey, Lekeitha, listen now").
- This song works well as a game for waiting times. Ask children to contribute with action words that they want to act out ("Hey, dear Christopher, jumping, jumping, hey, dear Christopher, jumping fine"; "Hey, my friend Omar, twirling, twirling, hey, my friend Omar, twirling fine").
- Toward the end, or when you need to stop moving, you can use this version:
  Hey, everybody, stopping, stopping,
  Hey, everybody, stopping now.

The Bear Track

Unknown Source | CD Track 47 | Song Card Page 102

Hands behind your back,

Hands behind your back,

[We're] [going] down the [bear] track.

Using the Song

Ask individual children what kind of animal they would each like to be. This can turn into a great opportunity for role-playing while moving. You can pretend that you're walking through the jungle or through the ocean. This chant is especially effective with very young children because it is short, clear, and fun. Its repetitive and consistent tempo helps the children participate even when you adapt it by adding new words.

Variations

▧   After you have used this chant for a while, choose other places for your children's hands ("Hands on your head," "Hands on your belly button," etc.).

▧   To personalize this chant further, ask each child where everyone's hands should go on his or her personal track:

Hands behind your neck, hands behind your neck,

We're going down Gabriela's track.

Riding in the Buggy

Traditional Folk Song | Adapted by Carol Aghayan | CD Track 48 | Song Card Page 102

A   E7   A
Riding in the [buggy], [Ms. Mary Jane], [Ms. Mary Jane, Ms. Mary Jane],

A   F#m   E7   A
Riding in the [buggy], [Ms. Mary Jane], a long way from [home].

A   D   A
Come [ride] with [me]. Come [ride] with [me].

              F#m   E   A
Come [ride] with [me], [my darling]. Come [ride] with [me].

A   E7   A
Riding on a [tractor], [Sean Michael], [Sean Michael], [Sean Michael],

A   F#m   E7   A
Riding on a [tractor], [Sean Michael], a long way from [school].

A   D   A
Come [fly] with [me]. Come [fly] with [me].

              F#m   E   A
Come [fly] with [me], [dear Rylan]. Come [fly] with [me].

Using the Song

Prepare children for this transition by asking them to think about how they would like to reach their destination. Ask them for their favorite way to move, and use them in this song (for example, "Hiking up the mountain, Ms. Natasha, Ms. Emma, Mr. Joel"). Be part of the turn-taking with children. This way you will help expand your children's vocabulary and offer something new that they might like to try next time.

Variations

- When you take ideas from the children, you might want to change part B slightly:

  Let's ride with Ayca, let's ride with Pierre,

  Let's ride with Oxum, my darling,

  Come ride with me.

- Adapt the end of the song to fit children's choices of how to move (for example, "Come hike with me").

Walk Along, John

Traditional | Adapted by Nina Araújo | CD Track 49 | Song Card Page 102

G
Come on, [children], and [hush your talking].

                D   G
All [join hands], and let's go [walking].

                  D   G
[Walk along], [André], with your [green pants on].

                  D   G
[Walk along], [Luc], with your [zebra shirt on].

Using the Song

This song offers a great way to keep children moving and having fun. You can change from walking along to hopping along and from marching along to jumping along very quickly. The children will also enjoy asking you to move in the funniest ways that they can dream up. Notice what they are doing shortly before you are getting ready to leave, and incorporate that information into the song (for example, "and hush your giggling"; "and meet me at the door"). If you are used to using other methods for walking with groups of children, substitute it for "all join hands" (for example, "all find a loop" or "all make a line"). Use detailed information about the children in the second part of the song (for example, "walk along, Jésus, with your water-walking Velcro shoes on").

Variations

- You can simply repeat the last lines until you have named all of the children in the group before repeating the first two lines. Remember to vary the actions: "hop along," "skip along," etc.
- Ask your children which animal they want to be for this trip, and use the animal names in place of the children's names.

Hop, Old Squirrel

Traditional | Adapted by Nina Araújo | CD Track 50 | Song Card Page 102

G   D   G   D
[Hop], [old squirrel], [eidledum, eidledum]. [Hop], [old squirrel], [eidledum, dum].

G   D   G   D   G
[Hop], [old squirrel], [eidledum, eidledum]. [Hop], [old squirrel], [eidledum, dee].

G   D   G   D
[Leap], [old frog], [eidledum, eidledum]. [Leap], [old frog], [eidledum, dum].

G   D   G   D   G
[Leap], [old frog], [eidledum, eidledum]. [Leap], [old frog], [eidledum, dee].

Using the Song

Empower children to choose how they will move to reach their final destination. Ask them what they want to do while singing "eidledum," and encourage everyone to follow their peers' ideas. Invite children to bring or become different animals. You can either leave it as an open choice or, if you notice that some children have been interested in particular animals, use this opportunity to remind them about those animals ("Let's bring mammals only today!"; "Let's bring striped and spotted animals only today!"; etc.).

Variations

- Change the sound for "eidledum" (for example, "heisseldum, heisseldum," etc.).
- Add your destination at the start, ask individual children where they are going, and quickly add this information to the song:

  Going to the playground, eidledum, eidledum.

  Luc is going, too, eidledum, dum.

  Wesley is coming, too, eidledum, eidledum.

  And Cameron is coming, eidledum, dee.
- Try using this song when saying goodbye:

  Affir's going home, eidledum, eidledum . . . (etc.)
- If you need to change the activity level or use it during slowing down times, try this version:

  [Sleep], [old squirrel], [eidledum, eidledum].

  [Sleep], [old squirrel], [shh, shh shh, shh].

  [Hush], [dear Amar], [eidledum, eidledum].

  [Hush], [dear Juniper], [shh, shh shh, shh].

Waiting

The children in Sara's class arrive at the cafeteria only to learn from the cook that the pizza won't be ready for another ten minutes. Sara pulls her song cards out and starts singing "Sarasponda" (CD track 55). All the children get involved, and when the pizza arrives, the children are still together in one group. Sara redirects them to pick up their "saraspizza."

Waiting times are often difficult for children and teachers alike. It's easy to lose focus as many times the children are left with very little direction as to what is coming next. They need to know what to expect and to predict what is going on while they are in school. It is inappropriate to expect children to wait without something to occupy their attention.

Even in Sara's high-quality program, whose schedule she carefully plans, there are times that waiting just happens. For example, since children eat at different paces, the ones who finish first need to wait for the teachers to give them direction as to what will happen next.

Sara uses her waiting times as community-building time. Unlike transitions that include a goal you want children to focus on (getting quiet or getting everything picked up, for example), waiting times can also be used for skill building and practicing concepts, such as phonemic awareness, notions of math and science, and problem-solving skills.

Tommy Thumb

Traditional | CD Track 51 | Song Card Page 103

[Tommy] [thumb] is up and (thumbs up) [Tommy] [thumb] is down. (thumbs down)

[Tommy] [thumb] is [dancing] (alternate thumbs in the air left, right, left, right)

All around the town. (alternate thumbs in the air left, right, left, right)

[Dance] him on your [shoulders]. (tap thumbs on shoulders)

[Dance] him on your head. (tap thumbs on head)

[Dance] him on your [knees] (tap thumbs on knees)

And tuck him into bed. (tuck thumbs into armpits)

[Polly] [pointer] is up and (pointers up) [Polly] [pointer] is down. (pointers down)

[Polly] [pointer] is [dancing] (alternate pointers in the air left, right, left, right)

All around the town. (alternate pointers in the air left, right, left, right)

[Dance] her on your [shoulders]. (tap pointers on shoulders)

[Dance] her on your head. (tap pointers on head)

[Dance] her on your [knees] (tap pointers on knees)

And tuck her into bed. (tuck pointers into armpits)

[Ruby] [ring] is up and (ring fingers up) [Ruby] [ring] is down. (ring fingers down)

[Ruby] [ring] is [dancing] (alternate ring fingers in the air left, right, left, right)

All around the town. (alternate ring fingers in the air left, right, left, right)

[Dance] her on your [shoulders]. (tap ring fingers on shoulders)

[Dance] her on your head. (tap ring fingers on head)

[Dance] her on your [knees] (tap ring fingers on knees)

And tuck her into bed. (tuck ring fingers into armpits)

Using the Song

This song helps children focus on the different names for our fingers and the various body parts we use for their "dancing." Be flexible, and ask children to make up their own finger dancing motions for this song. They will enjoy choosing a different name for each finger as well. This quick song helps your children also learn about listening and taking turns. Invite your children to create their own motions to this song—especially if you have older preschoolers in your classroom—by saying, "What would you do for pinkie finger?"

Many young children are challenged by the actual names for fingers. For seeing children, you can easily lift up the finger you are talking about, and they will be able to find the same in their own hands. If you have children who are either blind or visually impaired, they will need more direction as to which one you will be singing about. Encourage children to use detailed descriptors to locate a finger in your hand before you start singing the song (for example, "middle finger is between pointer finger and ring finger" instead of "here" or "there" or "this one"). At times you will need to touch children's hands to make sure they can participate.

Variations

- Ask individual children which finger they want to sing about.
- Ask for ideas about where fingers can dance (for example, "Dance her on the floor and dance her on your shoes").
- Ask children for different body parts that can dance (for example, "Lillian's knee is up, and Lillian's knee is down").
- Challenge children by making purposeful mistakes so they can "help" you with the words ("Dance him on your shoulders," but place fingers on your knee; "Pointer finger is up," but lift up pinkie finger instead, etc.).
- Randomly assign both genders to fingers. Make sure that you have a good balance between "he's" and "she's."
- Use children's names for the fingers instead:

    [Lillian] [pointer] is up and (pointers up)

    [Lillian] [pointer] is down (pointers down) . . .

Waiting

Join into the Game

Traditional | CD Track 52 | Song Card Page 103

E   B7   E
Let everyone [clap hands] like [Jane]. (clap your hands)

E   B7   E
Let everyone [clap hands] like [Jane].

    E7   A
Come on and join into the game.

    B7   E
You'll find that it's always the same.

Using the Song

You can repeat this song many times, making it especially suitable for waiting times. Depending on how long the waiting period is, you can invite children to participate by choosing actions. Of course, if you have any control over waiting times, plan ahead to prevent or minimize them!

Gesturing with your arms to invite children to participate shows children what you mean by the words "join into the game." Be sure to honor all ideas equally, and praise each child for his or her contributions.

Variations

- Ask individual children how they want to move so their friends can imitate their ideas (for example, "Let's jump up and down like Boudreaux"; "Let's hop on one foot like Jessi"). If they choose to do something that is inappropriate or unsafe, offer two alternate choices to help them learn about making positive decisions.

- At times, you might find it necessary to influence children's ideas toward calmer actions that lower activity levels ("Let everyone sit down like me"; Let everyone whisper like me"; "Let everyone wiggle toes like me"; "Let everyone blink eyes like me").

- If you are in an environment that has musical instruments available and easily accessible to your children, incorporate them into the song while you wait (for example, "Let everyone play sticks like Joel"; "Let everyone drum like Beth").

- You can also use this song at any time during the day to model and encourage appropriate behavior in the classroom ("Let everyone wash hands like me"; "Find a spot to sit like me"; "Let's clean up the block area like Sophie"; "Let's put blocks away like Laurie"). Personalize this song for your children, and expand it to as many transitions as you can. The only limit is your imagination!

Sticky Bubble Gum

Traditional | Adapted by Nina Araújo | CD Track 53 | Song Card Page 103

G
Sticky, sticky, sticky, sticky

            D   G
[Bubble gum, bubble gum, bubble gum].

Sticky, sticky, sticky, sticky

[Bubble gum].

D   G
Stick it to your [toes].

One, two, three! ("unstick" the sticky item!)

Using the Song

Encourage children to create sufficient individual space as they stick and unstick the bubble gum in this song. Ask children to contribute their ideas for motions that can be used for "sticky" and "bubble gum." Those motions will likely change periodically. Invite them to teach everyone how to count to three in their home language.

Variations

- Ask children to name other items that are also sticky. Have a list of possible ideas on your song card to expand on children's ideas (lollipop, maple syrup, glue stick, honeycomb, masking tape, etc.).
- Sing the song faster, then slow it down when the energy level reaches a point that you consider no longer healthy for the group.
- If some children are having a hard time sitting, tell them that the gum is magical, and ask them to stick it to their bottoms. Tell them that when you say a magical word, the gum will come off their bottoms, and they may get up. In this case, humor is an effective tool to guide behavior.

The Bog Down in the Valley-O

Irish Folk Song | CD Track 54 | Song Card Page 103

```
A           D           A              E
Oh, the rattlin' [bog]. The [bog] down in the [valley-o].
A           D           E              A
Oh, the rattlin' [bog]. The [bog] down in the [valley-o].
A                                      E
And in that [bog], there was a [tree]. A rare [tree], a rattlin' [tree].
         A                    D        E  A
Oh, the [tree] in the [bog], and the [bog] down in the [valley-o].
A                                      E
And on that [tree], there was a [turtle]. A rare [turtle], a rattlin' [turtle].
         A
Oh, the [turtle] on the [tree], and the tree in the [bog],
         D          E   A
And the [bog] down in the [valley-o].
```

Using the Song

This song is especially helpful during long waiting periods. Plan to be flexible and open to "silly" ideas ("the shark on the tree and the tree on your head and your head in the bubble gum . . ." etc.). The focus here is to help them feel engaged and have fun while waiting. Improvise motions for some parts of the song, or ask children for a motion that comes with an idea ("Dylan, what should we do for 'bog'?"). This engages their whole bodies in the song and gives them a way to participate when they forget the words. You might also want to think of a large motor movement to do when you sing the chorus in this song (for example, swinging arms while standing up and down) to break free from sitting down so much.

Variations

- Include landscape features that are characteristic to your geographical area ("the bayou in the swamp-o"; "the beach down by the ocean-o"; "the rocks down in the desert-o"; etc.).
- Hum the song while using only the gestures you've created.
- Sing most of the song softly, and when you sing the refrain, sing it loudly.

Sarasponda

Traditional | CD Track 55 | Song Card Page 103

```
     E                           B7
Sarasponda, sarasponda, sarasponda,

       E
Ret set set!

                              B7
Sarasponda, sarasponda, sarasponda,

       E
Ret set set!

       A      E      A          E      A
Ah doray oh. Ah doray boom day oh. Ah doray boom day,

  E
Ret set set.

B7           E
A say pasay oh.
```

Using the Song

This nonsense song can be used as a game to pass the time while waiting. You can pair children off to sing it as a clapping game, or you can all sing together making the same motions. The clapping game uses a basic clap-slap pattern for every word in the song, which consists of alternating clapping the hands and slapping a body part (most often the knees) while singing. For this song, you could follow the pattern: Saras (clap hands) ponda (slap knees), Saras (clap hands) ponda (slap knees), Saras (clap hands) ponda (slap knees), Ret set (clap hands), set (slap knees). Plan on changing this pattern every time you notice that your children need a new and enjoyable challenge while waiting!

Variations

- Choose different repetitive sounds to replace "ret, set, set" (for example, "boom, boom, bam," etc.).
- Every time you start the song, ask individual children for ideas for what to do at "ret, set, set."
- This song can also be used at dismissal times: sing each child's first and last names instead of "ret, set, set" to signal that they should leave the larger group and transition into the next activity (for example, "Sarasponda, Sarasponda, Sarasponda, Gillian Blair").

Waiting

Yapo

Traditional | Adapted by Nina Araújo | CD Track 56 | Song Card Page 103

A
Yapo. (Slap thighs) Y ya ya (Slap shoulders with arms crossed)

Ya ya yo. (Snap fingers at waist level from right to left)

Yapo. (Slap thighs) Ya ya (Slap shoulders with arms crossed)

Yay (Snap fingers at waist level from right to left)

Yapo. (Slap thighs) Ya ya (Slap shoulders with arms crossed)

F#m   D
Yapo. (Slap thighs) Y tooki tooki (Dance fingers on your head)

E   D
Yapo. (Slap thighs) Y tooki tooki (Dance fingers on your head)

A
Yay. (Snap fingers at waist level from right to left)

Using the Song

This nonsense song has a pattern of various body motions that are a lot of fun for older preschoolers. You will need to adapt them for younger children, who might be more comfortable starting with a simple clap-slap pattern. The repetitive and simple sounds inspire them to participate soon after they are introduced to this song. When you choose the motions for this song, keep in mind what you know about the children in your classroom, especially their developmental needs.

Variations

- Leave the words out and keep the motions in until you only have gestures and humming left.
- Sing the song in a different key.
- Change the speed, always remembering to ask individual children what they prefer to do when it is their turn.
- Incorporate a partner game with patterns such as thigh-clap-slap.
- Vary the volume: loud, soft, whisper, etc.
- Chant the song for a change.
- Try to make up a version with your children's names only. Mix in some parts of the original lyrics if you are running out of names:

  Christina, Rebecca, Andrew, Luc,

  Alexandra, ya, ya, yay. Anna, and Jack, and Lori

  Y tooki, tooki, yapo,

  Y tooki, tooki yay.

Here Sits a Shark

Traditional | Adapted by Nina Araújo | CD Track 57 | Song Card Page 103

G
Here sits a [shark] in [her] chair, chair, chair.

D   G
She lost all [her] [true sharks] she had last year.

G7   C   A7
So rise upon your feet and [greet] the first you meet—

D7   G
The [friendliest] one we know.

Using the Song

This musical game is especially useful for long waiting times and rainy days. Plan to have your children make a circle around one child who sits in a chair or on the floor (the "shark" in the chair). The circle walks around the child in the center while clapping hands or stomping feet, or both, and singing the song. When you sing, "so rise upon your feet," all stop clapping and moving so the center child can walk to the circle and choose a friend ("greet the one you meet") to be another animal in the chair. It is much easier for the center child to remember to stand up and choose a friend when the circle stops moving while still clapping and singing. Help your children choose one another for turns and avoid having some who are not selected. Try giving children turns to be in the middle by saying, "let's choose someone who hasn't had a turn yet."

Variations

- Ask individual children which animal they want to be and incorporate their ideas into the song.
- Some children like to add something to the line about "all her true sharks" (for example, "Here sits a shark in her chair, chair, chair; She lost all her true fish she had last year"; etc.).
- Other children might like to modify the "greet" portion of this song (for example, "and blink the first you meet") to make it silly. Go with the flow, and note their ideas on your song card so you can replay them when you use this song again ("Let's use Malcolm's idea this time!").
- After you play this game several times, try asking the child in the middle to give hints to the circle about which friend is taking the next turn (for example, "his name starts with 'L,' and he has a blue shirt on today").
- Some children might prefer that you sing their names instead of an animal's name.
- Ask your children for substitutions for "friendliest" (for example, "happiest," "greenest").

Aiken Drum

Traditional | Adapted by Nina Araújo | CD Track 58 | Song Card Page 103

        A   D
There was a [man] who lived in the moon,

A   E
In the moon, in the moon.

        A   D
There was a [man] who lived in the moon,

         E   E7   A
And [his] name was Aiken Drum.

        A   D   A   E
[His] [eyes] were made of [bubble gum, bubble gum, bubble gum].

        A   D
[His] [eyes] were made of [bubble gum],

        E   E7   A
And [his] name was Aiken Drum.

        A   D   A   E
[His] [hair] was made of [noodles, noodles, noodles].

        A   D
[His] [hair] was made of [noodles],

        E   E7   A
And [his] name was Aiken Drum.

Using the Song

This traditional song offers children infinite opportunities to let their imagination run free. Very young children sometimes have a hard time coming up with food items, and it might help them if you ask, "How about if his belly button is made with something that you have in your fridge at home?" Don't forget to use "she" for Aiken Drum sometimes too. If you think that's confusing, slightly change Aiken Drum's name, but keep either Aiken or Drum to make it familiar.

Variations

- If you have been talking about certain topics in your classroom, incorporate them and stretch their imaginations. For example, if you've been talking about ocean life, include every ocean item possible to "build" Aiken Drum's body: "His hair was made of sea anemones," etc.
- Change Aiken Drum's habitat to something that might be meaningful for you and the

children. You might ask children, "Where is Aiken Drum living today?" Keep track of their contributions, and be sure to give every child a turn with this song.

- You can also adapt this song to be used for saying good-bye to children at the end of the day:

There was a [friend] who lived in [Sedona],

In [Sedona], in [Sedona].

[Christina] is her name, and "good-bye" is the game.

We will see [her] again, I know!

[Good-bye]!

Say goodbye to each child in his or her home language or in any other way they prefer. Ask them beforehand to personalize this song and teach one another the many ways that we can say good-bye to our friends before they leave.

- Here's another way to adapt this song to use during dismissal times (especially if food is involved). When children hear their names, they choose a food item for their body to be made of and transition into the next activity:

There was a [friend] who lived in [Seattle],

In [Seattle], in [Seattle].

There was a [boy] who lived in [Seattle],

And [his] name was [Nathan Williams].

[His] [fingers] were made of [Nathan's choice: string cheese]

[String cheese], [string cheese].

[His] [fingers] were made of [string cheese],

And [his] name was [Nathan Williams].

Swimming Pool

Traditional | CD Track 59 | Song Card Page 103

C
Swimming, swimming (mimic swimming in a pool with both arms)

F   G   C
[In the swimming pool]. (draw a rectangle in the air to represent the swimming pool)

        F
When days are hot, (fan yourself with your hands)

        C
When days are cold, (wrap your hands around your upper body pretending you are cold)

F   G
[In the swimming pool]. (draw a rectangle in the air to represent the swimming pool)

 C   C7
Front strokes, (swim frontward with one arm) sidestrokes, (swim sideways with one arm)

 F   C
Fancy diving too. (hold your breath and pretend to dive into the pool)

    F   C   F   G   C
Wouldn't it be nice if there (face your hands palms up) was nothing else to do? But . . .

Using the Song

Sing this song with all the gestures to make it more interesting. Starting at the beginning, take one word out at a time while continuing to do the motions. Ask individual children which words you will take out at a time. It might help to hum the portion that was taken out when children are learning the song, especially if you have very young ones in your classroom.

Variations

- Vary the pitch (high and low) and the speed (fast and slow).
- After you and the children are comfortable with all the gestures in this song, make up new ones to add fun and extra challenge.
- Ask children for other places that are used for swimming, and incorporate this information into the song.
- Use this slightly changed version, if you want to add some children's names to the song: "Swimming, [Yuto], in the swimming pool . . ." etc.

Slowing Down

The children in Mr. Bordelon's classroom have had lunch and read some books. They are ready to look for their cots (always stored in the same place every day). Mr. Bordelon dims the light and wakes up his "naptime" puppet, which comes out of its basket only to wish the children good night. Mr. Bordelon starts singing, "Go to sleep my little Kenyan, and tuck in your toes . . ." (CD track 63) as he walks around the room, stopping at each cot so his puppet can give the child a kiss good night or a back rub as he reassures all of them that he will still be there when they wake up. Mr. Bordelon does not sing during the entire naptime, however. He uses his voice to welcome children into a new mood and to settle them in their cots, and then plays familiar lullaby recordings. This allows time for Mr. Bordelon to take notes on individual children, plan for the next day, or rejuvenate.

Calming times are opportunities for children to take a break from a busy schedule, unsettling issues, or the pressures of group life. Some children need only a reassuring glance, secure in the knowledge that their primary caregiver is nearby, while others need a little more time and physical proximity to their primary caregiver. This transition relies on rituals and a predictable sequence of events, especially for younger children; it's a great opportunity to help children learn about ways to slow down when the day gets busy (for example, after they finish eating lunch or when they need to renew their energies for the remainder of the day).

It's Time to Say Good Night

Camp Song | Adapted by Nina Araújo | CD Track 60 | Song Card Page 104

Em
It's time to say [good night].

G
The stars are shining bright.

Am   D
[At three] we'll see our friends again.

G   Em
Let's say good night 'til then.

Em
Here goes our [dear friend] [Sara].

G
We hope that [she] sleeps well.

Am   D
We all say ["See you in the morning!"],

G   Em
And [much later] we'll meet again.

Using the Song

This song works well with older preschoolers, who might not sleep during naptime but still need to rest their bodies. You can plan to sing it to each child as you walk around making sure that all are ready to rest (they have quiet toys, books, blankets, soft animals from home, etc.). If you use recorded music during this time, plan to have it ready to start after you transition the children into this quieter atmosphere. Ask children and their families about bedtime rituals and what words are used at home to wish each child "good night." Even though it is not evening time, invite children to join you in a "pretend" night rest.

Variations

- Change the first line to fit your transition or to include the words that you use to help children predict what is coming ahead (for example, "It's time to say 'see you soon'" or "It's time to find your mats").
- In line 5, use a variety of ways to refer to your children to individualize this song: "Here comes our lovely friend Bibi"; "Here comes our good old Lori"; etc.

Lord, Blow the Moon Out

Traditional | CD Track 61 | Song Card Page 104

Am   E   Am
Bed is too small for [Ayda's] tiredness.

Am   C   E
Bring [her] a hilltop of trees.

Am   E   Am
Tuck a cloud [up under] [her] [chin].

 C   E   Am
[Lord], blow the moon out, please.

Am   E   Am
Rock [Manuel] to sleep in a [cradle of leaves].

Am   C   E
Sing [him] a lullaby of dreams.

Am   E   Am
Tuck a [dinosaur] [up under] [his] [chin].

 C   E   Am
[Let's] blow the moon out, please.

Using the Song

Start this song by inviting children to "blow out" the lights in the classroom where they take their nap (turn the light switch off as they "blow"). After your room is darker, start singing this song, and ask each child where they want to tuck the cloud so they can rest (chin, hands, head, pillow, feet, etc.).

Variations

- If there are too many children for you to sing the entire song for each child, use a section per child (for example, "Bed is too small for Ben's tiredness"; "Rock Isabella to sleep in a cradle of dreams").
- Ask individual children where they would like to be rocked to sleep instead of a cradle of dreams, and incorporate this information into the song.
- If you don't use the word "Lord" in your program, you can substitute "let's" (see lines 4 and 8).

Are You Sleeping?

Traditional | Adapted by Carol Aghayan | CD Track 62 | Song Card Page 104

G
[Frére Jacques, Frére Jacques],

  C   G   C   G
Dormez-vous? Dormez-vous?

Sonnez les matines, sonnez les matines,

  D   G   D   G
[Ding ding dong, ding ding dong].

 G
Are you sleeping, are you sleeping,

  C   G   C   G
[Ashley Roya, Ashley Roya]?

[Morning bells are ringing, morning bells are ringing],

  D   G   D   G
[Ding ding dong, ding ding dong].

Using the Song

Use the English translation of the song first, if you only have English speakers in your group, but don't be afraid to learn and sing it in French too! In multilingual groups it is worth soliciting the help of families that speak languages other than English in their homes to rewrite this song in the children's home languages. Plan to ask individual children what "sleepy" sounds their morning (naptime) bells make, and use them to personalize this lullaby.

Variations

- Change "morning bells are ringing" to "naptime bells are ringing" when it is time to sleep, and use "morning bells are ringing" when it is time to wake up.
- Lower your voice and slow the tempo of the song slightly when you sing "naptime bells are ringing" as a way to signal to your children that it is their turn to fill in the blanks before they go off to rest.

Go to Sleep, My Little Pumpkins

CD Track 63 | Song Card Page 104

       A   D   E   A
Go to sleep, my [little] [pumpkins], and tuck in your [toes].

       A   D   E   A
Go to sleep, my [little] [pumpkins], you will turn into a [rose].

       A   D   E   A
Go to sleep, my [little] [Omar], and tuck in your [toes].

       A   D   E   A
Go to sleep, my [little] [Omar], you will turn into a [rose].

       A   D   E   A
Go to sleep, my [little] [Oliver], and tuck in your [toes].

       A   D   E   A
Go to sleep, my [little] [Sarah], you will turn into a [rose].

Using the Song

Start singing this song with the word pumpkin (or any other word you typically use to refer to young children, like sweetheart, sweet pea, honey) while the children are settling into their sleeping cots, finding a book to read, etc. The length of this song allows you to sing it to each child, regardless of how many "pumpkins" you have in your group. An effective accompanying ritual, especially with very young children, is to use a "naptime" puppet who wakes up to wish the children a "good rest time" and then goes back to sleep again after the song is sung to him or her.

Variations

- Ask individual children to share their bedtime rituals, and incorporate them into the song (for example, "Go to sleep, my dear Hyung Kyung, and cover your bed").
- It may reassure some children to sing this song to the family member he or she misses so much and to remind the child that the family member is resting now too. It may also be useful to have a photo album or a single picture of the child's family nearby to alleviate separation anxiety.
- Use a different body part each week or each month, and make up a new rhyme ("And tuck in your eye. . . . You'll fly like a butterfly" or " . . . You'll fly into the sky"; "And tuck in your knee. . . . You will turn into a bee").
- Use each child's favorite food item or lunch box edible, if he or she brings it to school ("Go to sleep my little tomato," " . . . my little tofu," " . . . my little sardine," etc.).

Baby Chant

Traditional | CD Track 64 | Song Card Page 104

A
Now it's time to go to [sleep]. (open your hands flat to be the bed)

D   Bm
Put [the baby] in the bed. (put your pointer finger on the hand to be the baby)

D   Bm
Cover [the baby] in the bed. (fold your fingers over the pointer in the middle of the hand)

(Keep adding going-to-bed rituals)

E   A
And [kiss] [the baby] [good night]! (kiss the top of your finger)

A   D   Bm
Now it's time to [go to sleep]. Put [Andreas] in the bed.

D   Bm   E   A
Cover [Andreas] in the bed. And kiss [Andreas] [buenas noches]!

A   D   Bm
Now it's time to [go to sleep]. Put [Michael] in the bed.

D   Bm   E   A
Cover [Michael] in the bed. And [kiss] Michael [nighty night]!

Using the Song

Use this song before you send children to their mats to rest or while they are settling in and shifting into a quieter mode; add children's ideas as they volunteer them. At times, you might end the song without ideas from everyone, if they fall asleep in the process. End the song with "And kiss everyone good night" or "And I'll blow you kisses good night." Help younger children participate by asking about what they do before nap (put toys away, wash hands, get blanket from cubby, etc.).

Variations

- Sing to individual children, and use one idea at a time instead of the string song format:
  Now it's time to go to sleep. Put [Jonah] in the bed.
  (Teacher: "What can I do before I kiss you good night, Jonah?") (Jonah: "Read a book")
  Read a book to Jonah
  And [kiss] Jonah [good night!]
- Adapt the first line in the song to make sense to your group (for example, "Now it's time to go to rest").
- Ask individual children what gesture they prefer to use to be sent to sleep (a hug good night, a high five good night, or anything else they are used to doing or saying at home.)

Slowing Down

Sleep, My Duckling

Finnish Folk Song | Adapted by Nina Araújo | CD Track 65 | Song Card Page 104

Am   Em Am Em
Sleep, dear [Amanda], [in the rushes],

 C   Am   E
While the winds are blowing.

 E7   Am   E   Am E
[Sunshine] will warm you, [waves] will cool you,

 Am E   Am
And I will care for and love you.

Using the Song

When you sing the last line in this song, try to be as physically close (in an appropriate way) as possible to each child. Don't rush through it, as its message of unconditional love has tremendous power for young children, who need to hear "And I will care for and love you" as often as possible. It will feel reassuring and comforting to many children who spend their days in school worrying about stresses from home.

Variations

- Try to find out in advance what imaginary place is dearest to each child, and then refer to these in the song (for example, "Sleep, dear Hamish, in your boat"; "Sleep, my Milena, in your castle").
- Add features from the natural world or the region where you live to personalize line 3 in this song: "Sunshine will warm you, and snow will cool you"; "The hot sun will warm you, and fall leaves will cool you"; "The spring sun will warm you, and breezes will cool you"; "Sunshine will warm you, and rain will cool you."

Slowing Down

Arrorro, My Baby

Argentinean Lullaby | CD Track 66 | Song Card Page 104

Am   A7   Dm
Arrorro, [dear Violet], arrorro, my own

E   E7   Am
Arrorro, my [lovely one], sunshine of our home.

               A7   Dm
Sleep will not come to [her], always runs away.

               E7   Am
Arrorro, [dear Violet], sleep is here to stay.

Using the Song

This Argentinean lullaby tells us about a child who is struggling to go to sleep, an issue familiar to many children. Rather than saying it is the child's fault that he or she can't fall asleep, this song playfully suggests that "sleep always runs away," taking the pressure off the children's shoulders and helping them relax during this time of day. Begin using "sleepy" signals right before you start singing this song to your children (for example, yawning, saying how tired you are, etc.).

Variations

- If you know what each child likes to be called, use that word instead in line 1, especially if there is a "home word" for dear in each child's house ("Arrorro, chère Selène"; "Arrorro, querido Pedrinho"; "Arrorro, Cariño"; etc.).
- Write on your song card many ways you can say "lovely one" to your children to make this song even more special to them, and make sure the card is available and accessible.
- If you cannot pronounce "arrorro" or if you want to change the way you sing this lullaby, hum the word instead.

Slowing Down

Good Evening, Shining Silver Moon

German Folk Song | Adapted by Nina Araújo | CD Track 67 | Song Card Page 104

       E
[Good evening], shining [silver moon].

 B7 E   B7
Where sail you there so high?

  E   A   F#m
I go to shine where [Frankie and Lyle]

   E B7 E
In [darkness lie].

Using the Song

This is a short song that can be used for two children at a time. Sing it for children who are next to each other so you can look and smile at them when you sing their names.

Variations

- Ask your children about what can fly up high and use it as a substitute in line 1 (for example, "Good evening, shining glittery star," ". . . magic kite," ". . . hot air balloon," etc.).
- In line 4, use places that are familiar to the children (for example, "on their cots they lie," "with their pillows they lie").

All the Pretty Little Ponies

Traditional | Adapted by Nina Araújo | CD Track 68 | Song Card Page 104

Gm
[Hush 'n' bye],

Cm
[Don't you cry],

D7
Go to sleep, my little [Yoran].

Gm
When you wake,

Cm
[You shall have] [cake]

D7
And all the pretty little [ponies]–

Dm
A brown and a gray,

Gm
A black and a bay,

Cm   D7   Gm
And all the pretty little [ponies].

Using the Song

Start by humming this song before you sing the actual words. After you have sung it a few times, children will recognize the melody and start anticipating hearing their names in it. Depending on the age of the children in your class, humming can also be a signal for them to go to their mats and wait until you come around to tuck them in. Plan to ask them what animals they would like to have when they wake up (imaginary, of course).

Variations

- Change the first two lines to something else every once in a while ("Time to sleep, my dear sheep"; "Head on your pillows, my dear willows"; etc.).
- Use line 5 to let them know what they will have for snack after they wake up (for example, "When you wake, you shall have juice and crackers").
- If you have something planned that you know they will love doing after they wake up, mention that as well when you sing lines 4, 5, and 6 ("When you wake, we will play in the water table and all the cups and buckets and sifters"; "When you wake, we will play with goop and read books from the library"; etc.).

Shady Grove

Traditional | Adapted by Nina Araújo | CD Track 69 | Song Card Page 104

Am   G
Shady grove, [my little love],

Am   G   Am
Shady grove, my dear,

Am   G
Shady grove, dear [Susannah],

Am   G   Am
I'm so glad you're near.

Am   G
[Sail] to the [sky] up high,

Am   G   Am
Or sail down the stream.

Am   G
Shady grove, dear [Kolya],

Am   G   Am
I'll see you in our dreams.

Using the song

Sing this song as you dismiss individual children to rest during naptime. If your center welcomes stuffed toys from home, encourage the children to have them along as you sing this song. When children hear their names, they quietly walk to their resting mats to rest for a while.

Variations

- Sing lines 3, 4, 7, and 8 only and hum the rest while you walk around tucking each child in.
- If you have time to sing the entire song to each child, ask each one to where he or she would like to sail, and incorporate the information into the song (for example, "Sail to the tree up high"; "Sail to the clouds up high").

Appendix A

Frequently Asked Questions

What's Inside This Book?

- A variety of songs with variations and adaptations for beginning and experienced teachers
- Suggestions on how to plan for your transitions, including a transition planning guide
- Suggestions for personalizing songs according to cultures, classroom, regions, and developmental needs of children
- Guitar chords for all the songs in this book
- Song cards teachers can use to "carry" the songs with them
- A companion CD with sixty-nine songs for seven types of transitions

We suggest variations for each song in this book. We offer them as starting points or as a way to keep them new and interesting to you and your children. Most of them grew out of some specific moment, motion, word, or wish. With each teacher and group of children something quite different may happen. We encourage you to pay attention to the children in your classroom and include your observations in your songs.

Why Are Some Words in Brackets?

All songs have words or whole sections in brackets. The brackets indicate opportunities for substituting the names of children in your classroom or words that come from the children or from your daily observations of what can make songs more interesting and meaningful for the children in your care.

How Can I Personalize the Songs?

- Change a word or two, or add a verse, a line, or a word to a song.
- Use body sounds like clapping or tapping your chest or thighs.
- Change the melody, or turn a song into a chant.
- Plan for improvisation. Children always bring something unexpected!

- Be spontaneous. Take risks.
- Spend time listening to the songs you don't know but want to learn.
- Let improvisations come from the children as much as possible.

How Can I Practice Spontaneous Music with the Children in My Classroom?

- Develop your own relationship with the song first: memorize the words and then find a rhythm or something fun that connects you to the music.
- Repeat, repeat, and repeat unfamiliar songs as many times as you want, until you and the children can sing and add variations to them.
- Invite children by starting to sing first. Don't ask them to repeat after you. Children will probably not sing with you right away, especially if the song you're singing is new to them. Begin singing or humming, and they will feel invited to join in immediately.
- Make eye contact with each child, and notice their reactions. Focus on what elicits an enthusiastic response to the song you are singing.
- Make eye contact with other adults in the room, so they feel included and comfortable and you don't feel alone.
- Mistakes happen; you don't need to focus on them or criticize them. They usually correct themselves quite naturally, and children will feel more comfortable participating in a criticism-free environment.
- Most important, have fun, and be sure to communicate your enjoyment to the children in your care.

How Do I Use the Chord Charts?

We have chord charts for all the songs in this book. However, it is not necessary to play an instrument to use transition songs with your children. We have them available for those who already play an instrument and might want to play them during some of the transitions. Simple percussion instruments (tambourines, egg shakers, etc.) can also add spice to your music.

How Does This Song Go Again?

Some songs are old favorites, and some will be new to you. We encourage you to use the CD to learn songs and use the song cards as a memory aid when you are in the classroom with children. If you normally share your songs with the children's parents, this is also a great way for them to learn the songs.

If the melody of a particular song seems too complex, you can always make up your own melody or use an old nursery rhyme as a substitute. You can also chant the words with body rhythms like in "Sarasponda" (CD track 55). We encourage you to use a clap-slap type of body rhythm (clap your hands and slap your thighs in a pattern).

A few familiar tunes are easy to sing, change, and rearrange, including "Twinkle, Twinkle, Little Star," "Jingle Bells," "Happy Birthday," and "Frére Jacques."

Song Cards: What Are They, and How Can I Use Them?

We have formatted the lyrics (see Appendix B) for your convenience. You can copy the pages and cut them apart to make song cards. Or you can copy them onto full-page copier labels and then cut them out and stick the labels on 3-by-5 cards. You might want to color code the cards in some way: by using a different colored card for each kind of transition (for example, blue cards for naptime songs, orange cards for greeting songs) or by adhering small stickers or swiping the cards with highlighters. They will last almost indefinitely if you laminate them! They are easy to store (in an index card box or on a ring—simply punch a hole in the corner of each card), so they can be easily accessed at all times. Carry them with you in your backpack or purse to jog your memory and help you learn new songs.

Appendix B

Song Cards

Good Morning to You

[Good morning, good morning],
[Good morning] to you,
[Good morning] to [someone]
Who's [wearing the color blue].

Good Morning, How Are You?

[Good morning], [Emillie]. How are you?
[Good morning], [Emillie]. How are you?
It will be a [special] day,
I'm so glad you came to play.
[Good morning], [Emillie]. How are you?

Hello, Everybody, Yes, Indeed

Oh [hello], [everybody], yes, indeed.
Yes, indeed. Yes, indeed.
Oh [hello], [everybody], yes, indeed.
Yes, indeed, [my darling]!

Sally, Go 'Round the Sun

[Celia] go 'round the [sun],
[Celia] go 'round the moon,
[Celia], [good morning] to you, [my friend],
We'll play [together] soon!

I'm Glad You Came Out Today

[Marwan O'Kiell] I'm glad you came out today, came
   out today, came out today.
[Marwan O'Kiell] I'm glad you came out today, 'cause
   we're gonna [have some fun].

Hickory Dickory Dock

[Hickory Dickory Dock],
[Annieck] ran up the clock.
The clock struck [one],
[Annieck] went home,
[Hickory Dickory Dock].

Good-bye; Don't Cry

Good-bye. [Don't cry.]
[Wipe a tear from your eye.]
Cheery up [ching ching]. Good-bye, old thing.
Boom diddy ah good-bye.
Before you go, I want you to know
It's been such fun,
[The things we've done],
Boom diddy ah good-bye.

What Shall We Do When We Go Home?

What shall [Don] do when [he] [goes home]?
What shall [Don] do when [he] [goes home]?
What shall [Don] do when [he] [goes home]?
When [he] goes [home today]?
[He'll have a snack] when [he] goes home.
[He'll have a snack] when [he] goes home.
[He'll have a snack] when [he] goes home.
When [he] goes home today.

Good-bye, Hey, Hey

[Good-bye], Katherine, [hey, hey].
[Tchau, tchau], Mônica, [hey, hey].
[Good-bye], Ella, [hey, hey].
[À bientôt], Juliette, [hey, hey].
We're gonna be right here when you come back,
We're gonna be right here when you come back,
We're gonna be right here when you come back,
Go'n' to be so happy here to see you back again.

Little Johnny Brown

Little Johnny Brown, lay your blanket down.
Little Johnny Brown, lay your blanket down.
Let's [say] [good-bye] to Seléne Motron.
Let's [wave] [good-bye] to Paddy Clancy.
Let's [bow] [good-bye] to Yeh-Eun Kyung.
Let's [say] [good-bye] to Johnny Brown.

From *Easy Songs for Smooth Transitions in the Classroom* by Nina Araújo and Carol Aghayan, © 2006. Published by Redleaf Press, www.redleafpress.org. This page may be reproduced for individual or classroom use only.

The More We Get Together

Oh! The more we get together, together, together.
Oh! The more we get together,
The happier we'll be.
There's [Tanya and Eric]
And [Emma and LaKisha].
Oh! The more we get together, the happier we'll be.

Baked a Cake

If I knew [you] were coming, I'd have [baked a cake],
[Baked a cake], [baked a cake].
If I knew [you] were coming, I'd have [baked a cake].
How-ja-doo, How-ja-doo, How-ja-doo.

Everybody Shake a Hand

Everybody [shake a hand],
[Shake a hand, shake a hand].
Everybody [shake a hand],
And [walk] around the room.

Stella Ella Olla

[Stella] [Ella] Olla,
Clap, clap, clap,
Singing esteega teega,
Teega, teega, shack, shack.
Esteega, teega, valo, valo,
Valo, valo, valo va,
One, two, three, four, five!

Over in the Meadow

Over [in the meadow], [in the sand, in the sun]
Lived a friend named [Sônia] and a friend named
  [Clara].
[Dance], said Sônia. [I'll dance!], said [Clara].
And they [danced] and they [danced] [in the sand,
  in the sun].

Bakery Shop

[Five] little [donuts] in the bakery shop
Looking so yummy with the [sprinkles] on the top.
Along came [Dylan] with a [penny] to pay.
He got this [donut], and he [walked] away.

Purple Stew

Making a [purple] [stew].
Making a purple [stubeedoobeedoo].
[Purple potatoes,
And purple tomatoes]
And [Logan] in the purple stew!

The Train Is a'Leaving

[The train] is a'leaving, oh yes.
[The train] is a'leaving, oh yes.
[Train] is a'leaving, [train] is a'leaving,
[Train] is a'leaving, oh yes.
Better get your tickets, oh yes.
[Luc] get your tickets, oh yes.
[André] get your tickets, [Pedrinho] get your
  tickets,
[Vitor] get your tickets, oh yes.

I Wonder What Tina Can Do

I wonder, I wonder, I wonder
What [Tina] can possibly do.
I wonder, I wonder, I wonder
What [Tina] can possibly do.
[She] can [play with blocks] or [paint at the easel]
Or maybe [play with some glue].
I wonder, I wonder, I wonder
What [Tina] can possibly do.

New Shoes, Old Shoes

[New] [shoes], [old] [shoes].
[Zirque] has some [new] shoes.
One, two, three, and four.
Tap them gently on the floor.

Do as I'm Doing

Do as [I'm] doing,
Follow, follow [me].
Do as [I'm] doing,
Follow, follow [me].

A Ram Sam Sam

A ram sam sam. A ram sam sam.
Guli guli guli guli guli. Ram sam sam.
[Arafi], [arafi].
Guli guli guli guli guli. Ram sam sam.
Stop, look, and listen. Stop, look, and listen.
Guli guli guli guli guli. Stop, look, and listen.
[Arafi], [arafi].
Guli guli guli guli guli. Stop, look, and listen.

Open and Shut Them

Open and shut them, open and shut them,
Give a little [clap, clap, clap].
Open and shut them, open and shut them,
Lay them in your lap, lap, lap.
Creep them, crawl them, creep them, crawl them
Right up to your chin, chin, chin.
Open up your little mouth
But do not let them in!

Put Your Finger on Your Nose

Put your finger on your nose.
And put your finger on your toes.
Put your finger on your lips.
And put your finger on your hips.
Put your finger on your knees.
Hands in your lap now, please.

Sit on Your Bottom

[Sit on your bottom] now just for me.
I love [you] and [you] love me.
That way we'll all be as happy as can be
By the time I count to one-two-three.
One, two, three.

Only One Can Talk at a Time

Only one can talk at a time
And this is what I'll do,
I'll sit as still as a little mouse
Until other folks are through.

A Little Bit Up

A little bit up, and a little bit down.
A little bit up, and a little bit down.
A little bit up, and a little bit down.
That's what makes the world go around.
I have two hands; I'm gonna make them move.
I have two hands; I'm gonna make them move.
I have two hands; I'm gonna make them move.
That's what makes the world go around.

Five Little Hotdogs

Five little hotdogs frying in the pan.
The pan got hot
And one went
BAM!

Five Little Peas

[Five little peas] in a [pea pod] pressed.
One grew, two grew,
And so did the rest
They grew and grew and did not stop,
Until one day they all went [POP]!

Two Little Houses

Two little [houses] closed up tight.
Let's open the [windows] and let in some light.
[Ten] little finger people tall and straight
Ready to sit down by the time I count to eight!

How About You?

[I] can [put the books away]; how about you?
[I] can [put the books away]; how about you?
[I] can [put the books away]; how about you?
How about you, [my darling]?

We're Gonna Clean

[We're] gonna [clean] when the [spirit] says [clean].
[We're] gonna [clean] when the [spirit] says [clean].
When the [spirit] says [clean]
[We're] gonna [clean] right along.
[We're] gonna [clean] when the [spirit] says [clean].

I Like the Way

I like the way that [Shawanda] is cleaning up
And [Jessica] is cleaning up
And [Ana] is cleaning up.
I like the way that [Andrew] is cleaning up
On this [Tuesday] morning.

Blocks Go to Sleep

[Blocks] go to sleep [on the shelf, on the shelf].
Hurry, [Luc], and put them over there.
Let's clean up, pick up,
Help our friend [Oliver].
[Blocks] go to sleep [on the shelf, on the shelf].

Tidy Up

Tidy up, tidy up, put the [toys] away.
Tidy up, tidy up, we're finished for today.
Tidy up, tidy up, put the [toys] away.
For we'll take them out again next time we come
to play.

There Was an Old Friend

There was an old friend, and [his] name was
[Geraldo].
Ching-a chang-a polly mitch-a cow-me-o.
[He] came to play and put things away.
Ching-a chang-a polly mitch-a cow-me-o.
[He] [put away blocks] and helped all around,
Around and around until there was nothing sitting on
the ground.
Ching-a chang-a polly mitch-a cow-me-o.

Cleaning Spirit

[Anna] has that [clean-my-classroom] spirit,
Right in [her] [head], [she's] got it,
Right in [her] [head], [she's] got it,
Right in [her] [head].
[Anna] has that [clean-my-classroom] spirit,
Right in [her] [head], [she's] got it,
Right in [her] [head] to sta-a-ay.

What Can You Clean, Ponchinella Funny Fellow?

What can you clean, Ponchinella funny fellow?
What can you clean, Ponchinella funny you?
[Luc] can [pick up puzzles], Ponchinella funny
fellow.
[Luc] can [pick up puzzles], Ponchinella funny you.

Pick Up

[Liani], [pick up, pick up] all the [toys] now.
[Sienna], [pick up, pick up] all the [toys] now.
All day long we work and play.
Now it's time to put them away.
[Milan], [pick up, pick up] all the [toys] now.

And We Hunted and We Found

And we hunted, and we hunted, and we hunted,
And we found
Some [books] [on the floor].
And then we looked around—lookee there!
[Some] [say] there are some [blocks], and others
say nay.
[Some] [say] there are some [markers] that we
need to put away—lookee there!

Get On Board, Little Children

Moving

I've got a friend that you all know
And [Jacintha] is her name.
I've got a friend that you all know
And [Maddy] is her name.
Get on board, [little children],
Get on board, [little children],
Get on board, [little children],
There's room for many a more.

We're on Our Way

Moving

[We're] on our way, [we're] on our way,
On [our] way to [play outside].
[We're] on our way, [we're] on our way,
On [our] way to [play outside].
When [we] go outside, [we're] gonna [ride the trikes].
When [we] go outside, [we're] gonna [ride the trikes].
[Russell], [he rides the trikes] like this.
[Russell], [he rides the trikes] like this.

This Train Is Bound for Glory

Moving

This [train] is bound for [glory],
[Olga] is bound for [glory],
[Ivan] is bound for [glory],
[Children] get on board.
No more [painting and gluing],
No more [painting and gluing],
No more [painting and gluing],
[Children] get on board.

Follow Me

Moving

Follow me, [Gábi], follow me.
Point to things that you can see.
Put your hand on top of your [head].
And point to something that is [red].

Jim Along Josie

Moving

Hey, [come along], Jim along Josie.
Hey, [come along], Jim along Joe.
Hey, [hop along, hop along] [children],
Hey, [hop along, hop along] [friends].

Betty Martin

Moving

Hey, [Betty Martin], [tiptoe, tiptoe],
Hey, [Betty Martin], [tiptoe] fine.

The Bear Track

Moving

Hands behind your back,
Hands behind your back,
[We're] [going] down the [bear] track.

Riding in the Buggy

Moving

Riding in the [buggy], [Ms. Mary Jane],
[Ms. Mary Jane, Ms. Mary Jane],
Riding in the [buggy], [Ms. Mary Jane],
A long way from [home].
Come [ride] with [me].
Come [ride] with [me].
Come [ride] with [me], [my darling].
Come [ride] with [me].

Walk Along, John

Moving

Come on, [children], and [hush your talking].
All [join hands] and let's go [walking].
[Walk along], [André], with your [green pants on].
[Walk along], [Luc], with your [zebra shirt on].

Hop, Old Squirrel

Moving

[Hop], [old squirrel], [eidledum, eidledum].
[Hop], [old squirrel], [eidledum, dum].
[Hop], [old squirrel], [eidledum, eidledum].
[Hop], [old squirrel], [eidledum, dee].

Tommy Thumb

Waiting

[Tommy] [thumb] is up and
[Tommy] [thumb] is down.
[Tommy] [thumb] is [dancing]
All around the town.
[Dance] him on your [shoulders].
[Dance] him on your head.
[Dance] him on your [knees]
And tuck him into bed.

Join into the Game

Waiting

Let everyone [clap hands] like [Jane].
Let everyone [clap hands] like [Jane].
Come on and join into the game.
You'll find that it's always the same.

Sticky Bubble Gum

Waiting

Sticky, sticky, sticky, sticky
[Bubble gum, bubble gum, bubble gum].
Sticky, sticky, sticky, sticky
[Bubble gum].
Stick it to your [toes].
One, two, three!

The Bog Down in the Valley-O

Waiting

Oh, the rattlin' [bog].
The [bog] down in the [valley-o].
Oh, the rattlin' [bog].
The [bog] down in the [valley-o].
And in that [bog], there was a [tree].
A rare [tree], a rattlin' [tree].
Oh, the [tree] in the [bog],
And the [bog] down in the [valley-o].

Sarasponda

Waiting

Sarasponda, sarasponda, sarasponda,
Ret set set!
Sarasponda, sarasponda, sarasponda,
Ret set set!
Ah doray oh.
Ah doray boom day oh.
Ah doray boom day,
Ret set set.
A say pasay oh.

Yapo

Waiting

Yapo. Y ya ya
Ya ya yo.
Yapo. Ya ya
Yay
Yapo. Ya ya
Yapo. Y tooki tooki
Yapo. Y tooki tooki
Yay.

Here Sits a Shark

Waiting

Here sits a [shark]
In [her] chair, chair, chair.
[She] lost all [her] [true sharks] she had last year.
So rise upon your feet
And [greet] the first you meet—
The [friendliest] one we know.

Aiken Drum

Waiting

There was a [man] who lived in the moon,
In the moon, in the moon.
There was a man who lived in the moon,
And his name was Aiken Drum.
[His] [eyes] were made of [bubble gum, bubble gum,
    bubble gum].
[His] [eyes] were made of [bubble gum],
And his name was Aiken Drum.

Swimming Pool

Waiting

Swimming, swimming
[In the swimming pool].
When days are hot, when days are cold,
[In the swimming pool].
Front strokes, sidestrokes,
Fancy diving too.
Wouldn't it be nice if there
Was nothing else to do? But . . .

It's Time to Say Good Night

It's time to say [good night].
The stars are shining bright.
[At three] we'll see our friends again.
Let's say good night 'til then.
Here goes our [dear friend] [Sara].
We hope that [she] sleeps well
We all say ["See you in the morning!"],
And [much later] we'll meet again.

Lord, Blow the Moon Out

Bed is too small for [Ayda's] tiredness.
Bring [her] a hilltop of trees.
Tuck a cloud [up under] [her] [chin].
[Lord], blow the moon out, please.
Rock [Manuel] to sleep in a [cradle of leaves].
Sing [him] a lullaby of dreams.
Tuck a [dinosaur] [up under] [his] [chin].
[Let's] blow the moon out, please.

Are You Sleeping?

[Frére Jacques, Frére Jacques],
Dormez-vous? Dormez-vous?
Sonnez les matines, sonnez les matines,
[Ding ding dong, ding ding dong].
Are you sleeping, are you sleeping,
[Ashley Roya, Ashley Roya]?
[Morning bells are ringing, morning bells are
   ringing],
[Ding ding dong, ding ding dong].

Go to Sleep, My Little Pumpkins

Go to sleep, my [little] [pumpkins],
And tuck in your toes.
Go to sleep, my [little] [pumpkins],
You will turn into a rose.

Baby Chant

Now it's time to go to [sleep].
Put [the baby] in the bed.
Cover [the baby] in the bed.
And [kiss] [the baby] [good night]!

Sleep, My Duckling

Sleep, dear [Amanda], [in the rushes],
While the winds are blowing.
[Sunshine] will warm you, [waves] will cool you,
And I will care for and love you.

Arrorro, My Baby

Arrorro, [dear Violet], arrorro, my own
Arrorro, my [lovely one], sunshine of our home.
Sleep will not come to [her],
Always runs away.
Arrorro, [dear Violet],
Sleep is here to stay.

Good Evening, Shining Silver Moon

[Good evening], shining [silver moon].
Where sail you there so high?
I go to shine where [Frankie and Lyle]
In [darkness lie].

All the Pretty Little Ponies

[Hush 'n' bye],
[Don't you cry],
Go to sleep, my little [Yoran].
When you wake,
[You shall have] [cake]
And all the pretty little [ponies]—
A brown and a gray,
A black and a bay,
And all the pretty little [ponies].

Shady Grove

Shady grove, [my little love],
Shady grove my dear,
Shade grove, dear [Susannah],
I'm so glad you're near.
[Sail] to the [sky] up high,
Or sail down the stream.
Shady grove, dear [Kolya],
I'll see you in our dreams.

Appendix C
Sample Transition Planning Guide

TIME	ACTIVITY
Transition	Greetings and Good-byes ["Hello, Everybody, Yes, Indeed" and "Good-bye, Hey, Hey," CD tracks 3 and 9]
7:30–9:30 AM	Arrival, Breakfast, and Free Choice Time
Transition	Cleaning Up ["Cleaning Spirit," CD track 37]
9:30–9:45 AM	Cleanup
Transition	Gatherings and Dismissals ["The More We Get Together," CD track 11] ["Purple Stew," CD track 17]
9:45–10:10 AM	Morning Meeting Time and Snack
Transition	Gatherings and Dismissals ["Bakery Shop," CD track 16] Moving ["Walk Along, John," CD track 49]
10:10–11:10 AM	Bathroom and Going Outside
Transition	Moving ["Get On Board, Little Children," CD track 41]
11:10–11:20 AM	Cleanup and Inside
Transition	Gatherings and Dismissals ["Baked a Cake," CD track 12]
11:20–11:45 AM	Story
Transition	Gatherings and Dismissals ["Purple Stew," CD track 17]
11:45 AM–12:15 PM	Hand Washing, Lunch, and Preparing for Nap
Transition	Gatherings and Dismissals ["Stella Ella Olla," CD track 14] Greetings and Good-byes ["Good-bye; Don't Cry," CD track 7]
12:15–1:00 PM	Midday Meeting, End of Half Day, Toileting, and Outside
Transition	Moving ["Walk Along, John," CD track 49] Slowing Down ["Go to Sleep, My Little Pumpkins," CD track 63]
1:00–3:00 PM	Rest Time
Transition	Cleaning Up ["Cleaning Spirit," CD track 37]
3:00–3:20 PM	Cots Away and Snack
Transition	Moving ["Betty Martin," CD track 46]
3:20–4:20 PM	Outside
Transition	Moving ["Betty Martin," CD track 46]
4:20–4:45 PM	Inside and Free Choice
Transition	Cleaning Up ["Cleaning Spirit," CD track 37] Greetings and Good-byes ["Little Johnny Brown," CD track 10]
4:45–5:15 PM	Cleanup, Stories, and Good-byes

TIME	ACTIVITY
Transition	
Transition	
Transition	
Transition	
Transition	
Transition	
Transition	
Transition	
Transition	
Transition	
Transition	
Transition	
Transition	
Transition	
Transition	

Index of Songs